Signs of the times 83
Sensitivity 85
Non-verbal communication 88

90 PRODUCTION
Pinhole cameras 92
Photography 94
Storyboard 98
Tape recorders 100
Animation 103
Animation without a camera 103
Animation with a camera 105
Video 108

112 REPRODUCIBLE MATERIAL

124 GLOSSARY

126 RESOURCES

127 OTHER SCHOLASTIC BOOKS

128 ACKNOWLEDGEMENTS

Introduction

Bright Ideas

Media Education

Written by Avril Harpley

Published by Scholastic Publications Ltd,
Marlborough House, Holly Walk,
Leamington Spa, Warwickshire CV32 4LS

Written by Avril Harpley
Edited by Christine Lee
Sub-edited by Anne Faundez
Designed by Sue Limb
Illustrated by Jane Bottomley
Artwork by Liz Preece,
Castle Graphics, Kenilworth.

Printed in Great Britain by Loxley Brothers Ltd, Sheffield

© 1990 Scholastic Publications Ltd

All rights reserved. This book is sold subject to the condition that it shall not, by way of trade or otherwise, be lent, hired out or otherwise circulated without the publisher's prior consent in any form of binding or cover other than that in which it is published and without a similar condition, including this condition, being imposed upon the subsequent purchaser.

No part of this publication may be reproduced, stored in a retrieval system, or transmitted, in any form or by any means, electronic, mechanical, photocopying, recording or otherwise, without the prior permission of the publisher, except where photocopying for educational purposes within a school or other educational establishment is expressly permitted in the text.

British Library Cataloguing in Publication Data
Harpley, Avril
 Bright Ideas : media education.
 1. Great Britain. Primary schools. Curriculum subjects.
 Mass media
 372.8'3

ISBN 0-590-76296-6

Front and back covers designed by Sue Limb.

Contents

4 INTRODUCTION

10 IMAGE ANALYSIS
Tell the story of a picture 13
Looking at me 15
Extend the frame 17
Photo story 20
Captions 21
Viewpoint 22
Associations 24

26 ADVERTISEMENTS
Ads, ads everywhere 28
Looking critically 30
Type of advertisements 32
Looking at the language 33
Ads around the world 34
Maths in ads 36
Television advertising 38
Design your own advert 39
Preparing an ad for TV 41

42 WATCHING TELEVISION
Why watch TV? 45
How do we watch? 48
What's past is past 50
Soap operas 52
Deep in soap 54

56 THE NEWS
Inside news 59
News views 60
Read all about it! 61
Whose news views? 63
My news, your news 64
Past news 67
Talking heads 69

72 COMMUNICATION
Is that really me? 77
Postman Pat 79
Is there anybody there? 81

WHY LEARN ABOUT THE MEDIA?

The media is the major communicator in our society – never before have we had access to such instant information and entertainment. It is also the major influence on our way of life, shaping our attitudes and opinions.

Children are bombarded by the media from birth and are vulnerable to its attractions, a constant stream of colour, excitement and emotional involvement. They choose to view television often for long periods at a time; they receive examples of behaviour, family life and society; ideas of race, culture, power, possessions and sexual mores. They learn about their own status in the world.

All too often television provides the bulk of their imaginative experience; it is action-packed and exciting. Some children believe that the world they see in the media is the real world, and on their own they do not have sufficient experience to make informed judgements. Media education extends children's understanding of the media and creates more active and more critical media users and producers. They become 'media literate'.

Every medium is a language of communication; it can be oral or written, aural or visual. Communication can be through print, drama, music, dance, painting, or any combination of these. Every medium has been constructed or produced by an author. The reader or viewer of the text, the audience, interprets the text according to his own, highly individual experiences.

Media-educated children are more capable of dealing with life in the technological world of satellite and cable TV, videos, computers, desk-top publishing and camcorders; they have an increased awareness and are able to make informed judgements. Media-educated children are better equipped to communicate in a variety of ways to suit a range of different audiences and purposes. They have a better informed choice.

MEDIA EDUCATION IN THE PRIMARY SCHOOL – USING TELEVISION

Motivation is the key factor in learning, and children are highly motivated by television. They are confident, in fact they are experts, often watching several hours a day. The main purpose of a teacher in the primary school is to help children to think for themselves, by making decisions and choices which enable them to mature and be valued as individuals.

In media studies the teacher's role becomes more of an adviser and organiser, setting up projects and guiding by careful questioning. By listening and directing, the teacher can feed in materials and ideas which extend the children's involvement. It is very important that the teacher does not place value judgements on the children's viewing; instead children should be helped to discriminate – to prefer good to poor, excellent to good. In other words, we should help them to develop good taste but not force our taste upon them. Children can learn to be critical and question what they see and hear. They may even become selective in their viewing habits, watching with a reason or a purpose; they may learn ways to express themselves creatively. This does not mean that their pleasure or enjoyment will be less, for, with knowledge, they may enjoy their favourite programmes even more. They can learn to construct a programme for themselves. Their critical awareness and skills may spread to other work areas.

STARTING POINT

Talking about television is a very good starting point. It is a highly pleasurable activity in which everyone's point of view is valuable, where there is no feeling of failure and no tests to worry about. The children are familiar with the content matter. It is within their experience and it bridges the gap between school and home.

Media education provides new and unusual ways of doing the basics. It does not mean starting a whole new area of work, learning new skills or buying expensive technical equipment. There are simple inexpensive ways of introducing it into the existing curriculum and programmes of study. It is an ideal way to present work and provide evidence for assessment.

The more able children will set themselves challenges and stretch themselves. The less able may gain a sense of achievement that they may not have in the traditional subjects.

HOW TO TEACH MEDIA EDUCATION

Use the children's knowledge of TV, print and packaging, posters, stickers, advertisements, comics, films and videos, fads, fashion and the merchandising of toys. Take into account the influence of brothers' and sisters' opinions, body language and conventions.

Children have been exposed to a whole range of sophisticated media texts. They are experts at watching TV yet are not being taught how to read it. There are simple low-tech ways of using their interests in the classroom.

Firstly, look at the media and learn to deconstruct it.

Secondly, let the children use media techniques to record and present their classwork.

MEDIA IN ANY THEME

Media education is not just another subject to add to an already crammed curriculum. It is more of an approach, a way of asking relevant questions. It encourages the children to think and question for themselves. Many of the topics I have suggested will fit in with the National Curriculum programmes of study that are proposed for the core subjects and will give you an alternative way of recording and presenting children's work.

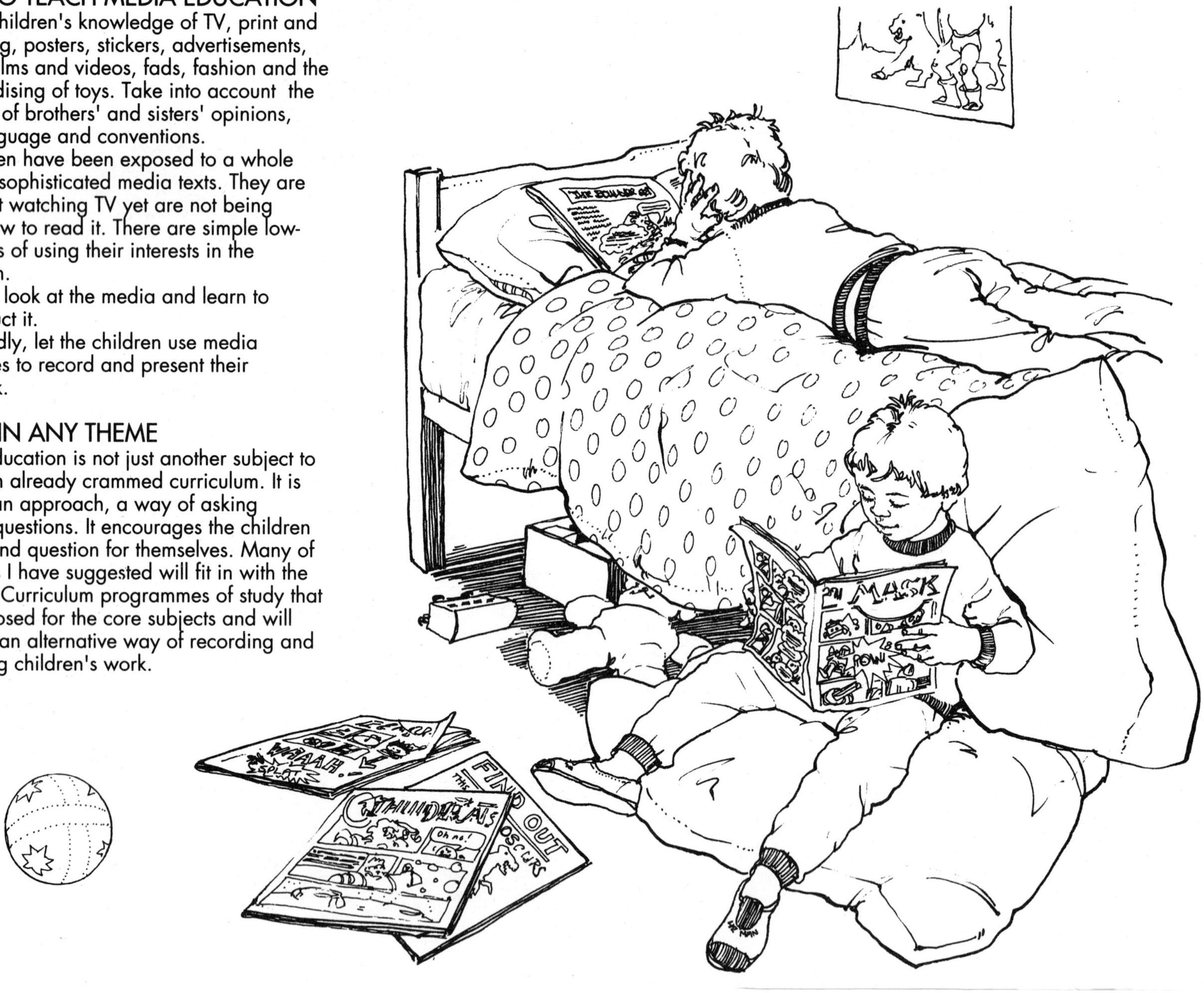

NATIONAL CURRICULUM ATTAINMENT TARGETS

Many of the activities suggested in this book can provide openings into areas of the science programmes of study, such as persistence of vision, lenses and magnification.

It is difficult to pinpoint specific Attainment Targets, as much of the work could develop out of the children's own interests. It is possible to cover many different areas. Keep an open mind: you may find Attainment Targets you didn't expect.

Some of the projects, such as video, animation or newspapers, can be studied in considerable depth with sophisticated results, but on a simpler level they are also within the reach of the youngest children.

I feel that English underpins most of this kind of work. The National Curriculum gives no clear guidelines for role-play, the use of visual narrative or the ability to 'read' the storyline of a soap opera. However, the media can be involved in most Attainment Targets.

There may well be unexpected hazards and problems with equipment. As with any unfamiliar area, try to plan ahead. Arrange for the equipment in advance and check whether you need batteries, plugs or lights. Limit the working groups and be clear about who will be in charge of the equipment.

Above all, do not be frightened that the children will not be able to cope. Children are nearly always keen to explore today's technology; they can be experimental, creative and confident.

Image analysis

Learning to decode visual clues and to deconstruct the image helps children to learn to read the media. Sometimes images can carry messages not always easily expressed by words, such as moods and emotions, while the position of images can influence our understanding.

Photography and film-making encourage children to think carefully about what they want to appear in their picture and why they want it there. They become the media agency, the producers of the text.

Media skills to be developed

Agency
Different agencies have different criteria and different purposes.

Categories
Different equipment produces different results. A still camera freezes action while a cine camera enables you to make cartoons and a video camcorder allows you to go out on location and view the film immediately.

Media language
We draw on our perceptions and knowledge of media codes and conventions to interpret the visual clues. In a Western, a close-up shot of a hand hovering on the gun holster prepares us for the 'shoot out'. Cutting from one scene to another lets us know that the action is happening simultaneously.

Technology
With a camera lens it is possible to alter the focal length and zoom towards an object or subject. It is possible to film from a great distance and to magnify a small object.

Representation
Children should become aware of what has been specially chosen to be in a picture, and also what has been deliberately left out. For example, in the carefully arranged scene in a holiday brochure of smiling, tanned young people sipping cool drinks around the pool, do we see the dustbins or rubbish dump behind the hotel?

Tell the story of a picture

Age range
Five to seven.

Media skill
Language: children should learn that photographs are planned and arranged.

Group size
Whole class, especially when using slides, or small groups, pairs or individuals.

What you need
Photographs, slides or pictures, paper, pencils, felt-tipped pens.

Audience
Knowing who will be looking at your picture will influence what goes into it. In this way, it will attract its intended audience. However a different audience may interpret the picture in quite a different way. Parents watching *He Man* will not be as motivated as their children. Children may not be as interested in a documentary on the political situation in South America as a businessperson with clients there.

This section on visual analysis gives simple ideas for group and class work that will promote discussion, the development of language strategies such as explaining, describing, justifying, naming and comparing, and the use of the imagination.

What to do

Ask the children to look carefully at a picture. Examine it in three parts: the background, the middle and the foreground. By questioning, try to find all the clues that give the picture meaning. What is the picture trying to say? Ask who, why, where, what and how. Can the children tell where the camera operator was standing? Do the people in the picture know they are being photographed?

Try to imagine what happened just before the photo was taken. What will happen afterwards?

Let the children draw their ideas. Ask them to write suitable captions to tell the story.

The children will realise that a great deal of planning goes into producing a picture.

Looking at me

Age range
Five to seven.

Media skill
Audience: the children should learn that different audiences will respond to various media in different ways.

Group size
Small groups or individuals.

What you need
Photographs of the children, their families and friends, display materials.

What to do
Make a display of the photographs and discuss them with the whole class. The display could be linked to another project, such as one on growth, change or time.

Ask why the photos were taken. Were they taken by a member of the family, or by a professional? Were the people in the photograph aware that the picture was being taken?

What is in the background? Have the people dressed specially for the occasion? Did they comb their hair? What time of the day and year is it? Is it a special event or celebration?

Can they remember how they were feeling? Can they remember what happened before the picture was taken or what happened afterwards?

Where was the photographer standing? Are they looking at the camera?

Categorise the photographs according to age, holidays, parties, festivals, outings, family occasions, seasons, portraits, groups, friends, babies or scenery. Ask the children to think of other possible categories.

Ask the class to choose their favourite photo. Why is it their favourite?

Extend the frame

Age range
Five to seven.

Media skill
Language: children will learn how the use of close-ups emphasises everything in the frame.

Group size
Groups of four to six children, pairs or individuals.

What you need
Objects with view-finders such as cameras, binoculars and telescopes, cardboard, scissors, paper, drawing and colouring materials, a selection of pictures cut from magazines.

How would the children choose to have their photographs taken? What would be the reasons? How would they choose a photograph for mum, for Gran, to show their friends, to have at school, to keep in a record book and to put on a Christmas card?

The children will become aware that photographs are taken for a variety of reasons. Different people looking at the same photograph will not necessarily have the same response to it.

What to do

Let the children explore the collection of view-finders. Ask the children to make a framing device by cutting a square out of the centre of a piece of card. Ask them to hold the frame at arm's length and describe and draw what they see. Ask them to hold the frames close to their eyes. What has changed? Experiment with looking at objects at unusual angles. Make frames in a variety of shapes.

Cut some pictures out of magazines, cutting away most of the background but leaving just enough to provide some clues. Stick the pictures on to sheets of A4 paper. Where you position them on the paper may dictate how the children perceive they should be interpreted. If you stick a picture close to one edge it may indicate that there is a great deal to be fitted into the centre and opposite side. If you stick it close to the top it may mean filling in lots of foreground.

Ask the children to use any clues left in the picture and draw in what they think has been cut from the rest of the picture. They need to focus on the details they can see and also to draw upon their own experience and knowledge of places and situations.

Alternatively, cut out a shape from anywhere in a picture and ask the children to draw in what is missing.

Explain to the children that photographs are often cropped for use in a newspaper. Cutting off some of the surroundings can give the subject more impact. Try cropping some pictures. Does it give a different meaning to the picture?

The children will learn that a photograph freezes time and space. It can be used to focus attention on to something specific.

Photo story

Age range
Five to seven.

Media skill
Agency: learning how to put images together to create meaning.

Group size
Groups of three or four children.

What you need
A collection of pictures or photographs, large sheets of backing paper, adhesive.

What to do
Give each group a selection of between six and eight pictures and ask them to consider each picture carefully. Discuss it on its own and also in relation to the others in the set. Can the picture's position affect its meaning? Let each group arrange the pictures on backing paper to make a story, then stick them in place.

Follow-up
An extension of this project could involve an editing process. Give the group ten pictures each and ask them to reject four.

The children should be aware that choices have to be made to produce a media text. It can be interesting for the children to take their own photographs when they go out on a school visit. They may like to have a theme, a particular sequence or a story line. The important point is that they plan what they want to do.

Captions

Age range
Six to eight.

Media skill
Language: the children should be able to understand simple visual narrative structure.

Group size
Individuals and small groups for discussions.

What you need
A selection of newspapers or magazines and comics, preferably non-English language, scissors, adhesive paper.

What to do
Choose a newspaper picture containing at least three people and cut off the caption. Make photocopies so that each group has the same picture. Ask the children to imagine what the people are saying. Compare the results.

Viewpoint

Age range
Five to eight.

Media skill
Representation: children should recognise there are differences in the representations of the same subject. Interesting work can be done by looking at the same situation from different points of view.

Group size
Pairs or individuals. Small groups for drama/role play.

What you need
No special equipment.

Why did the children interpret the picture the way they did? Try to elicit as many answers as the photo will permit. Look for clues and details.

Repeat the activity using comics, blocking out the words in the speech bubbles. Ask the children to write or tell the story from the picture. Do their interpretations differ?

Use this activity to introduce the concept of storyboarding. Storyboarding is the visual presentation of material. It is the planning tool for films, advertisements and animation. It highlights the key points of the story, ensures that the storyline makes sense and gives instructions for everyone involved in the production.

The children will come to understand that all parts of a media text have meaning and are there for a purpose.

What to do
Use well-known fairy tales and stories as a starting point. How did the poor old lady who lived all alone in the forest feel when two young children came and started to pull her house down? What about the large lonely man who had no friends – only a harp, a chicken and a few coins – who was then robbed and killed by a cheeky young lad?

Ask the children to retell a familiar story such as *Little Red Riding Hood* from a different viewpoint; Red Riding Hood's mother, the wolf, the grandmother.

Witness
Ask a group of children to enact a simple scene in front of the class. Divide the class into groups and ask them to discuss what they saw. Collect the different versions. Who was right? Is there a right answer? What did the role-play group think they were saying and doing? Why did they remember certain things and forget others? How can anyone be sure what happened?

What does it mean?
The same thing can mean something different to another person. Ask the children to discuss the following:
- What is snow to a polar bear, a child, a motorist?
- What is fire to a wolf, a traveller, a forest ranger?
- What is a tree to a squirrel, a carpenter, a wood louse?
- What is water to a child, a fish, a plant, a dirty sock?

Children should be aware of the fact that experience and involvement can influence response to a situation. They influence the producer's choice of a media text as well as the audience's reading of the text.

23

Associations

Age range
Four to six.

Media skill
Language: children will begin to understand codes and conventions which will help them later in interpreting visual clues.

Group size
Whole class.

What you need
No specific requirements.

What to do
Very young children often have some difficulty in holding two or more concepts in their minds long enough to examine and compare their attributes and therefore can find it difficult to follow a storyline with several facets. Use one or more of the following ideas to help develop this faculty:
• Play a simple word association game by asking the children what they think of when they hear a certain word.

- Ask the children to name specific furniture for a bedroom; a kitchen; a living room.
- Ask a child to describe a familiar animal or television character without naming it and let the rest of the class attempt to identify what or who it is.
- Ask the children to name appropriate articles of clothing for specific weather conditions or activities. Give the children a list of pieces of clothing and ask them to spot which is the odd one out, eg football shirt, wellington boots, socks, shorts.
- Ask the children to spot verbal or pictorial absurdities, eg a bed in the kitchen or a bicycle with square wheels.

Advertisements

How do companies make us choose to buy their products? What devices do they use to reach a particular group of people? The ideas in this section can be used to create a one-off assignment or expanded to become a whole term's project. They can be adapted to suit the whole primary age range.

Media skills to be developed

Agency
Advertisements are made by people, and someone is in control, with the final say as to what an advertisement will contain.

Categories
Children should learn to recognise different forms of advertisement and be able to tell the difference between information and selling. They should know what you can, or cannot do or show in different categories of advertisement, whether radio, TV or print.

Media language
Children should know that a scene is set up and constructed specifically for an advertisement. Decisions are made to achieve the final image of a product.

Technology
Children should be able to tell the difference between live action, animation and drama. They should understand that special effects can change reality. They should know the following vocabulary: shot, frame, close-up, location, focus. They should learn to operate equipment and use the facilities available.

Representation
Children should be able to distinguish between reality and fantasy and be able to say how they would represent the product.

Audience
Children should be aware of their own reactions as consumers and know that advertisements are targeted at a specific group of people with a set of common interests or goals.

Ads, ads everywhere

Age range
Five to eight.

Media skill
Audience: children should become aware of the way in which consumer goods are targeted towards a certain audience.

Group size
Whole class, then groups as specific interests develop.

What you need
Notebooks, portable tape recorders, tapes, cameras and film if you wish to record images, copies of photocopiable page 113.

What to do

Visit a local market, shop or supermarket with the children. Ask the shop manager if the children might make a note of the goods on offer and what people are buying. You may like to ask people about their purchases and, if they agree, record their answers using photocopiable page 113. Why do they choose a particular brand of goods? Take photographs of shop displays, the contents of supermarket trolleys and publicity hoardings.

On return to the classroom, make a collection of packages, labels, toys, and fashion fads such as stickers, badges and erasers. Younger children could turn their play corner into a shopping area with trolleys, baskets, a till and writing material to make lists.

The children should become aware of the variety of responses to and preferences for the goods on offer. Ask them whether age, gender or social class can influence choice. Get them to interpret their findings in graphs, sets and bar charts and discuss the results.

Looking critically

Age range
Five to eight.

Media skill
Categories: to be able to differentiate and identify media forms.

Group size
Whole class.

What you need
A collection of advertisements from a variety of sources.

What to do
Let the class take a critical look at an advertisement. What sort of text is it? Is it a drawing or a photograph? Does it show live action or is it a cartoon? Is there a story implied in the picture or is it a straight picture of the product? Does it appeal to the emotions? Does it encourage competitive feelings, for example, 'I must have that to be like everyone else'?

How can we tell that it is an advertisement and not drama or a cartoon? Can we recognise an advertisement? What are the visual clues? Are the eyes looking at the camera? Are the clothes of the model telling us about the lifestyle? What clues do we get from the location of the set? What is it trying to sell? Who is trying to sell the product?

Everything is in the picture for a purpose. Who has made the decisions? When looking at an advertisement on television, consider the style, the shots, the timing of the scenes (are they fast and slick, slow, dreamy, evocative?). How can you tell how many cameras were used? What techniques have been used to achieve the atmosphere? Long shots, close-ups, soft focus, music?

Does it give a real, honest view of the product? Does it claim that the product has super powers or produces amazing results? How are these claims made — by comparisons, scientific studies, people's recommendations or research?

At what time of day is the advertisement broadcast, or what type of newspaper or magazine does it appear in? Who are the viewers or readers? Try to find examples of an advertisement that is presented in different ways, depending on the media form. Does it change its form or style, depending on whether it is presented as a label, a poster or on TV? Who might buy the product?

The children should be aware that the text can be categorised in a number of ways. It can be drama, news, a cartoon, a documentary, print or film. Some material suits certain categories better than others. Certain factors govern different presentations.

Type of advertisements

Age range
Seven to nine.

Media skill
Categories: children should be able to recognise different forms of advertisements and texts.

Group size
Whole class.

What you need
Selection of media texts.

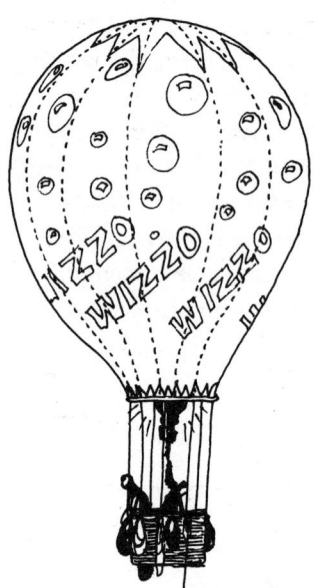

What to do
Make a list of examples of different types of advertisements. The list could include shop demonstrations; leaflets; posters; technical, special interest, hobby, fashion and glossy magazines; newspapers; shop window displays; radio; TV; teletext; promotions using gimmicks such as hot-air balloons, sports backing, clothes and logos.

Discuss the differences between a soft sell, such as an author talking about a new book on a chat show, a tennis star using a certain racket and information given on *Tomorrow's World*, for example, and a hard sell, such as when a double-glazing firm telephones you at home to sell its products.

Think about how you would sell a new TV show.

Compare the way in which books are advertised.

Does an advertisement change according to the medium used? What would be difficult to promote on radio? What could be done better on radio?

Children should be aware that the choice of medium affects the presentation, each has its own specificity and language. Some have more impact than others. Can the children find examples to show this?

Looking at the language

Age range
Six to eight.

Media skill
Representation: making judgements about reality.

Group size
Whole class working in small groups.

What you need
Lots of newspapers and magazine advertisements from a variety of sources.

What to do
Distribute the advertisements to the groups for discussion and questions. Analyse the words used. Are they descriptions, comparisons, superlatives? Note how few words are used to put over an idea, especially when it is linked to a visual clue. Mix captions from different

Ads around the world

Age range
Seven to nine.

Media skill
Representation: there can be different representations of the same people and objects.

Group size
Whole class working in small groups.

What you need
A collection of advertisements from a variety of sources, including some from other countries and some which are non-English language.

advertisements. What difference does it make? Remove the words and ask the children to make up their own. These can be humorous, show the product in a different light or make it appeal to a different audience. Make a list of words that appear frequently. Take an advertisement from one magazine and stick it in a totally different one, eg put an advertisement for *My Little Pony* in a technical magazine. Does this alter it in any way? Encourage the children continually to ask what message is being conveyed.

The children should be aware that producers often intentionally alter reality, eg the scale of the set may create the illusion that a toy is bigger than it is. Language is used to cement the visual messages.

What to do
Give each group a selection of advertisements and ask them to choose one for discussion. Can they find one important thing to say about it? Do advertisements from other countries differ from those in this country? If it is in a language other than English, can you tell what the advertisement is saying, what message it is trying to put over?

Are some products the same in all, or some, of the countries? Coca Cola sells all over the world: do they use different advertisements for it in India, Brazil, China and the United States?

Look at the advertisement critically. What has not been said about the product? Advertisements are a good starting point for looking at and discussing other lifestyles, stereotypes, wealth, health, sex, cleanliness, fashions, cultures and the influence of the Western world. What image of our lifestyle is portrayed? Is it a true picture?

The children should realise that audiences can make different judgements about the same text. Knowledge and experiences affect the way you read the advertisement.

Maths in ads

Age range
Seven to nine.

Media skill
Agency: children should learn that there are authors and producers of advertisements.

Group size
Whole class, then working groups of five or six children.

What you need
A collection of advertisements from magazines, comics and newspapers, a collection of commercial product labels and packaging, scissors, adhesive, backing paper, television, stopwatch.

What to do
Make a survey of the advertisements in your collection. Do any match up with the packets the children have seen on display (see page 29)?

Collect brand names and labels. Cut them out and make a display of them. What do they tell us about the product, its contents and weight? Do they tell us what we want to know? Sort them into sets, different styles or categories. Sort into food and non-food.

Compare the prices of the magazines, papers and comics. Compare the number of pages. Count how many pages are advertisements. What percentage of the whole is devoted to advertisements?

Time the length and frequency of advertisements on television. You may need the co-operation of parents to do this. Compare different viewing times: weekends, tea time etc. Is there a difference in advertisement saturation? Investigate claims like '15 per cent more, nine out of ten owners prefer...'. What do they really mean?

Find out how much it costs to place an advertisement in a newspaper or magazine. How much space do you get for your money?

The children will become aware that companies need to sell their products and that they use the media in a variety of ways. They pay to advertise. Newspapers, magazines, comics and independent television companies need the advertising money to help run their companies.

Television advertising

Age range
Seven to nine.

Media skill
Language: children should learn to recognise the conventions of certain media forms.

Group size
Whole class initially, then working groups.

What you need
Television, video cassette recorder.

What to do
Record a television advertisement and view it several times in succession. Notice how the words and images are linked. What sort of sets have been constructed? What sort of characters are portrayed? How many changes of scene are there? What is the pacing and timing like? Is it fast, exciting, slow and dreamy, bright and breezy? What shots are there? Are there close-ups or long shots? If any of these factors were changed, how would it affect the whole advertisement?

Collect word lists associated with the advertisement you are deconstructing. Which words are used to describe the product? Which tell you how good it is (for example, bigger, better, stronger, faster, cleaner)?

Introduce role play and ask groups of children to assume

the roles of a typical television family and introduce a product. What would they say? What sort of scene would you need to set up to sell the product? Try alternative ways of looking at it. Each group can take a different view of the product and a different style of presentation.

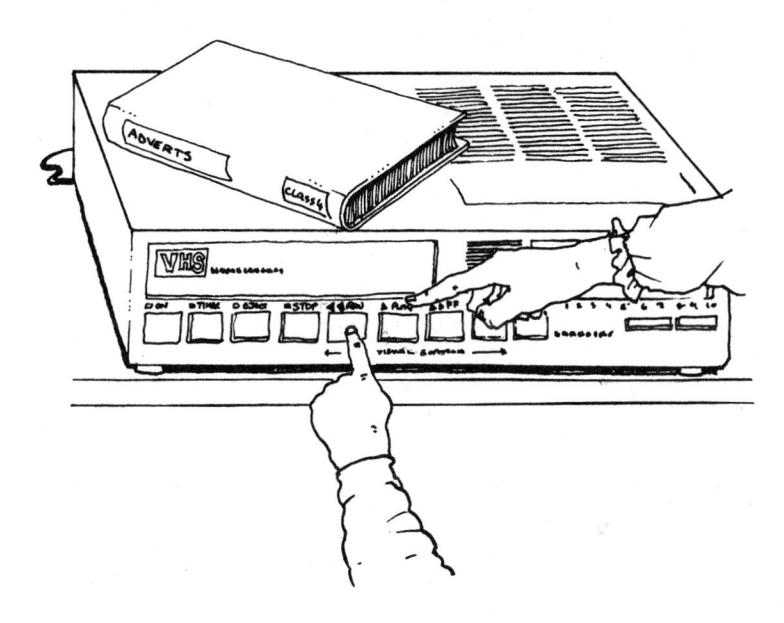

Listen to the sound and music accompanying the advertisement. What images do they make you think of? Try watching without the sound, or with a different soundtrack. Does your perception of the images change? Try with the sound only: can you identify the product? Do you get different images? How do the jingles match up with the pictures?

The children will come to understand that all the parts of the text have been put there for a purpose. The advertisement has been constructed by a group of people working together.

Design your own advert

Age range
Six to nine.

Media skill
Technology: the children should have the opportunity to make decisions about which technology to use.

Group size
The whole class for discussion, then small groups of three to six children.

What you need
Paints, felt-tipped pens, pencils, paper, camera, tape recorder, tape, camcorder.

What to do

Ask the children to design an advertisement to attract new parents to the school. It could be low-tech, for example like a poster, a booklet or a slide/tape presentation. It could be a radio broadcast, an animated film or a video. It could be in the form of a soft sell or it could be hard-hitting. It could be a friendly interview or a chat show. Try to find different angles, viewpoints and styles. Bear in mind the audience you are trying to reach. What would hold their interest? Consider the design of advertisements: do they follow a pattern? What sort of colours, shapes, techniques are used to conjure up the image?

Alternatively, take a well-known advertisement and redesign it, using a different medium. Does it have the same impact? Give yourself certain restraints, eg size, number of colours and shape of paper. Give the groups a time limit within which to work.

One group could act as the clients or owners of the product, one as the editors/producers, one as the designers and another group as the consumers. How difficult is it to please everyone?

The children will realise that technological choices make a difference to meaning. Presentation and style can affect the way in which the message is received.

Preparing an ad for TV

Age range
Seven to nine.

Media skill
Audience: children should be able to produce a media text for a specific audience and learn to use the appropriate equipment.

Group size
Six to eight children.

What you need
Pencils, paper, felt-tipped pens, timer, musical instruments or pre-recorded music, access to video cassette recorder.

What to do
Ask the class to prepare a television advertisement. Encourage them to consider who will be the audience, the consumer of the product. This may dictate the image they wish to promote, the words and pictures they will use, the price range of the product and the age and economic group of the consumer, the whole style of the advertisement and where they will advertise.

Ask them to write the script first, then to plan the storyboards including the colours to be used, pictures and layouts. Choose the sound, music or jingles to accompany the visuals. Keep to a total screen time of 25 seconds. Discuss the finished plans. Film some of the ideas (see Production).

The children will be aware that knowledge of the intended audience affects what goes into the text and that audiences are often targeted by companies.

Watching television

Television offers a wonderful opportunity to bring together knowledge, experience and pleasure without displacement or great expense. It can stimulate conversation, improve our taste and widen our experience of other countries' cultures and political ideas, thereby helping to make us less prejudiced and more tolerant of others. Used well, it can provide a good balance of entertainment and education. It can provide a strong emotional involvement and enrich the imagination.

On the other hand, television can be like a dripping tap, with constant moving pictures only half understood, the viewer watching with a glazed stare whilst idly flicking from channel to channel. It can seduce the viewer with fast action and over-stimulation of images. It can frighten children and keep them from going to bed. It can produce stereotypes and biased viewpoints. It can influence our thinking, our attitudes and the way we spend our money.

Media education respects each person's choice, but asks him to reflect on what he is watching: it encourages more informed choices.

Media skills to be developed

Agency

Children should know that television programmes are made as a result of a great deal of planning by a large number of people. They should be able to give a job description for basic production roles.

Categories
Children should be able to identify the different types of programmes, the media forms (news, documentary, drama, magazine, advertising, etc) and the genres (soap opera, adventure, musical).

Media language
Children should begin to recognise media conventions: the way presenters speak to the camera, titles, introductions and music, how the camera techniques help the narrative and can create suspense.

Technology
Children should be able to tell the difference between live action and animation. They should have some idea of how special effects have been created.

Representation
Children should be able to make judgements about the reality of what they see on television. They should understand that there may be many different viewpoints on a subject.

Audience
Children should be aware that there are different responses to television programmes, and they should learn to respect others' preferences.

Why watch TV?

Age range
Four to seven.

Media skill
Audience: children should know that there is a wide variety of preferences and that programmes appeal to different people for different reasons.

Group size
Small groups and individuals.

What you need
Drawing materials, modelling clay, scrap materials for making puppets.

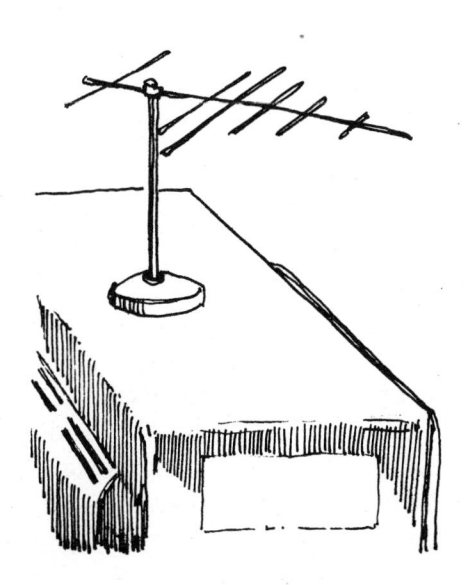

What to do
Organise discussion in small groups and ask open-ended questions about the children's viewing habits that require answers other than yes and no. For example, what did you do after tea last night when you returned from school? What do you prefer, playing in the rec, playing with toys, reading a book, watching television or having friends round? Why?

How many television sets do you have at home? Do you watch TV alone, with your parents, with friends? Do you have arguments about what to watch and when to watch? If so, how do you resolve them? Does your television have a remote control? If so, who holds the remote control?

When the children talk about their favourite television show they bring into use many language skills: recall, narrative structure and character description. They are learning conversation skills, patterns and strategies.

Ask the class to make representations of their favourite characters in drawings or in modelling clay. Make sure that the characters are placed in the appropriate surroundings, together with any special equipment that they use. Compile a list of words connected with the characters.

Alternatively, ask groups to make puppets and to enact a scene with them. They will have to decide which characters will be represented, where the action takes place and how the action will develop. Discuss character development. What sort of person is the puppet meant to be? Does he do good or bad things? Does he have friends, family or a special helper? Does he use super powers, strength or cunning? Does he make you laugh or cry?

Discuss the heroes. Do they follow a pattern? Make a checklist of their attributes. Are they clean-shaven, handsome, strong, tall, blond, kind, intelligent? Do they always triumph? Do they have a wife and children? Do they ever cry?

Then look at the 'baddies'. Do they follow a pattern? Can you always tell if a character is good or bad? If so, how? Ask the children to make up their own characters based on their knowledge of stereotypes.

The children should be aware of the fact that there are many responses to programmes and that people enjoy or dislike them for a variety of reasons. Programmes are made to suit different people.

How do we watch?

Age range
Five to nine.

Media skill
Audience: children should consider how television relates to their everyday life and their habits.

Group size
Small groups for discussion.

What you need
Notebooks, pencils, video cassette recorder, graph paper, felt-tipped pens, copies of photocopiable pages 114 to 116.

What to do
Ask the children to keep a diary of the programmes they watch over a period of time. Ask them to comment on the programmes rather than just writing down the titles.

Ask them to consider the following points:
- What are their preferences? Is there a pattern to their viewing?
- Do they watch television in the same place and at the same time of day? Where is their television situated?
- Do they watch alone, with peers or with their family?
- Do they do other things while watching television, such as eating, reading or model-making?
- Do they select programmes? Do they switch off when the programme has ended?
- What do they think about the way in which the programmes are scheduled? Does scheduling make a difference?

- Do they like children's television? Have the producers got it right?
- Is there anything special they would like to see on television or anything they would like to have changed?

Encourage them to write to a producer about a programme with their views and comments.

Ask them all to watch a particular programme and compare their responses. Suggest they watch something different or new that they do not normally watch. Ask them to try to find something interesting to say about it.

The results of the children's diaries can be presented in sets and graphs showing the programmes that are the most popular, the patterns and times of viewing. Add up the hours viewed throughout the week. How much is that a month, a year? What percentage of a day is spent watching television? Time the duration of the advertisements. Can the children predict when the next one will interrupt a programme?

Video ten minutes of a schools' broadcast and use it as a memory game. Watch it next week, then next month. Make a list of things to look for. What did you remember? Were there things that everyone forgot?

Ask the children to conduct a survey throughout the school using the questionnaires on photocopiable pages 114 and 115. Translate the information into graphs using photocopiable page 116.

The children should be aware of the diversity of choice available. What makes a programme attractive to them and why do they watch it?

What's past is past

Quote from a four-year-old: 'Miss Harpley, were you born before the world was coloured?'

Age range
Five to seven.

Media skill
Technology: children should know that there have been great changes in communication during the last 100 years and that television has not always been part of our everyday life.

Group size
Whole class.

What you need
Access to libraries, both print and film. Portable tape recorders, tapes, notebooks. Arrange a visit to a film museum.

What to do
Ask the children to find out what people did before they

had television. Encourage them to prepare a list of questions to ask elderly relatives or older people that they know. Are people still doing the same activities? Have some pastimes disappeared altogether? What did families do during the winter evenings? What is the approximate age of the people who grew up without television?

Try to watch some of the first children's programmes which are now available on video. Have children's programmes changed in any way? Do they still have something to offer to children today?

Visit a film museum such as the Museum of the Moving Image in London or the National Museum of Photography, Film and Television in Bradford.

Try to find some old box cameras to show the children. Make a pinhole camera (see page 92). Try to borrow a video camcorder from your Teacher's Centre. Compare the different equipment and techniques.

The children will become aware that television is changing all the time. New technology allows for greater freedom and creativity.

Soap operas

Age range
Six to eight.

Media skill
Categories: children should be able to recognise the different types or genres of programme.

Group size
Groups of approximately six children.

What you need
Pencils, paper, magazines, scissors, adhesive.

What to do
The television soap opera is one of the most seductive forms of viewing. They have huge ratings, with faithful followers watching them over a period of many years. Usually they present a view of family life and show the relationships between the family and the community and the problems and changes that occur. The events portrayed are easily recognised and understood by the viewers.

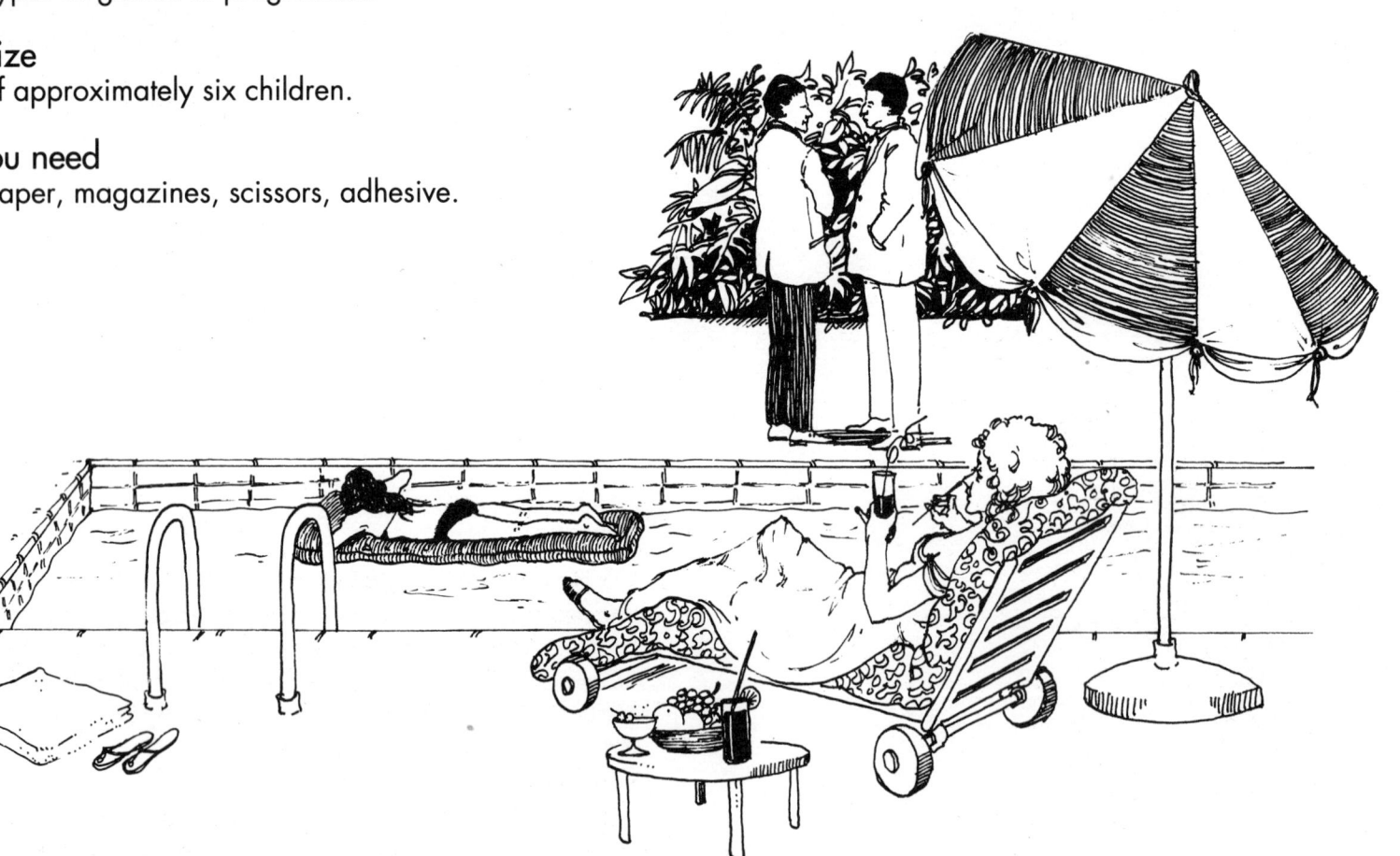

You can begin to explore the genre of soaps by considering how they are constructed: multiple story lines, interweaving of the characters' lives, familiar settings, continuous dramas with the suspense of a never-ending story-line.

Start by making a list of the characters and their relationships with others. Draw their family trees, including as much information as possible. Decorate the family trees with drawings or with pictures of the actors cut from magazines. Make another list of locations and sets. Where do the characters live, meet, work and play? Make an analysis of the characters. How do they see themselves, and how do they see each other?

Write the script for a soap. Decide on the scenes, the characters, the relationships and the setting. Is it about a family, a group, a place? Will the style be light-hearted? Will it convey a power struggle, a crisis, or an everyday story? Ask the children to draw pictures to accompany the soap opera.

Follow-up
Make a simple card game using soap opera characters. Make four sets of cards showing characters, their qualities, locations and style of drama.

Organise the children into small groups and give each child one card from each of the first three sets. Turn over one card from the style set, then let each group make up a story using the elements they have been given.

The children will learn that programmes can be classified into different categories and that there are conventions for media forms and genres that help you to recognise the different categories.

Deep in soap

Age range
Seven to nine.

Media skills
Representation: children should query how real is the 'real life' on television.
  Language: children should be able to recognise the use of different features in a visual text.

Group size
Small groups for discussion.

What you need
No special equipment.

What to do
Discuss in class an episode from a current popular soap opera that the children have watched. Allow them to compare ideas and encourage them to listen to each other's viewpoints. Ask them to think about how the programme began. Can they draw a series of pictures to show the beginning? Does the programme give a résumé of the previous episode, or does it show the characters in their settings? Does it pick the story up straight away? What sort of music is used in the introduction? If you missed the previous story, would you be able to follow what has happened? How? What happens if you switch on in the middle of an episode of an unfamiliar soap? How can you tell that it is a soap? Is there a beginning, a middle and an end?

How is the story told? How are drama and tension built up? How does it end? How does the producer show action happening at the same time in different places? How are transitions from shot to shot made (fade, cut, wipe, dissolve)? Using their knowledge of the series, can they make a guess as to what might happen next week?

    Soaps can also form the basis for discussion about families, lifestyles and cultures. Soaps can provide children with the experience of knowing about different environments, alternative lifestyles, places and conditions of work. Discuss the role of women in the families in programmes as different as *Dynasty* and *East Enders*. How are the young people portrayed? How do they cope with too much money, or none at all? Where does the action take place? What values and attitudes are shown towards other people?

    The children will realise that there are many different kinds of programmes. They can distinguish between them by looking at the way they have been made, how they begin and end, and the type of text they have. Point out that the real life shown on television is the producers' view, not necessarily the only view.

The news

People seem to have an insatiable desire for news, from international politics to juicy bits of gossip over the garden fence. The mass media provide the range, packaged in a variety of styles to suit a variety of audiences. You only need to look at the shelves in a newsagents to see the extent of interests and the choice available. There are local evening and weekly papers, dailies catering to every taste and monthly current events magazines. All of us are interested in items that concern us personally, and children are becoming increasingly aware of world-wide concerns such as the environment and ecology.

Media skills to be developed

Agency
Children learn by doing. By making their own newspaper, they learn about the tasks involved and the choices that have to be made.

Categories
The news is presented in different ways, depending on whether it is presented in newspapers, magazines, current affairs programmes, documentaries, news slots or as in-depth profiles. The presentation affects the way we respond to a programme (for example, *Spitting Image* or *Panorama*).

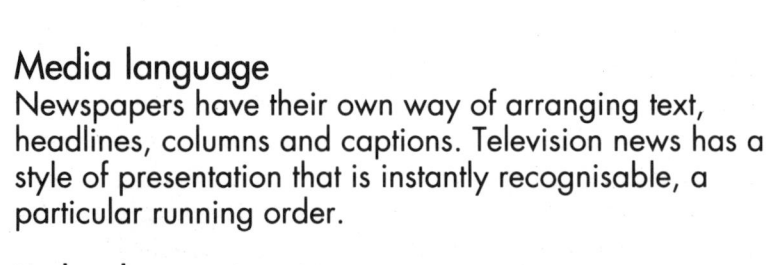

Media language
Newspapers have their own way of arranging text, headlines, columns and captions. Television news has a style of presentation that is instantly recognisable, a particular running order.

Technology
The arrival of lightweight video cameras and desk-top publishing has revolutionised the way news is collected.

Representation
How real is the news? Is the news constructed like a story? Can the same news be shown in different ways?

Audience
Children should question why news broadcasts are scheduled at certain regular times of the day. They should explore the reasons why people buy different newspapers and magazines.

Inside news

Age range
Seven to nine.

Media skill
Agency: children should be able to find out about the organisation that is involved behind the news, the variety of jobs involved and the role that each person plays.

Group size
Whole class, splitting into small groups to investigate specific areas.

What you need
Portable tape recorders, tapes, cameras, notebooks, pencils, access to a computer or typewriter.

What to do
Arrange a visit to a local newspaper office. Before going, the children should try to find out about how a newspaper works so that the visit has more impact. Give the children certain tasks and questions to answer. Each group could be responsible for finding out about a certain aspect of newspaper work and could then report it to the rest of the class. Ask them to look out for newspaper jargon and special vocabulary.

Back in the classroom, get the children to form groups and write up an account of the visit, using different styles and giving the story different slants or viewpoints. Appoint an editor for each group to check the work. Type the edited work. If cameras and tapes have been used, edit the material and decide upon the final selection.

The children should be aware that there are many people employed in the production of a newspaper. Many decisions need to be made before the news is printed.

News views

Age range
Six to eight.

Media skill
Representation: children should learn that there are different ways of seeing the world.

Group size
Groups of no more than six children, whole class for discussion.

What you need
Pencils, paper, felt-tipped pens, camera, newspapers.

What to do
Give the class a topic for a newspaper report such as coverage of an event at school (eg sports day, parents' evening), or a familiar story like *The Pied Piper*, *Humpty Dumpty* or *Goldilocks and the Three Bears*.

Ask each group to tell the story in a different way, but make sure that their stories all contain the same basic facts. The story could be told in the form of:
- A sensational story;
- A story that will induce sympathy;
- A shock horror story;
- A fun story;
- A complaint.

Get the children to illustrate their stories with drawings and photographs.

As a whole class discuss the different viewpoints and decide what makes them really interesting and convincing. Look at the newspapers and discuss news items. What are they really saying? Try to find the same story in different papers. Are there any differences?

The children will come to understand that people have different viewpoints which affect what they select to tell us.

Read all about it!

Age range
Five to seven.

Media skill
Language: children should learn that there are recognisable features such as variations in the typeface and print size of newspapers.

Group size
Individuals.

What you need
Captions and headlines cut out from a variety of newspapers, the corresponding stories, sheets of paper, adhesive, scissors, pencils.

What to do

Give the children a selection of headlines and ask them to match them up with the correct stories. Alternatively, give the children just the headlines and ask them to write and draw a story to match. Next, give them just a story or picture and ask them to write a suitable headline or caption. Let the children cut out letters and words from newsprint to make headlines for their work.

Ask them whether the caption changes the meaning of the picture. Does the news on television have headlines?

The children will realise that there are certain conventions of style and layout in a newspaper. Headlines catch our eye, capture our interest and lead us into a story. They give the 'feel' of the story.

Whose news views?

Age range
Six to eight.

Media skill
Representation: children should learn that there can be choices about how they represent themselves and others.

Group size
Pairs.

What you need
Portable tape recorder, tape, pencils, paper.

What to do
Explain to the children that interviewing is a technique that needs practice and that the interviewer controls how the conversation develops by what questions are asked. It requires a great deal of thought and forward planning and encourages awareness of others, such as how to approach people, co-operation and consideration.

Ask the children to form pairs, with one as the interviewer and the other as a character from a well-known story, such as Humpty Dumpty in hospital or Jack's mother describing the giant beanstalk. Make sure the children know their role and why they have been chosen to be interviewed. The interviewer should have a clear idea about what needs to be found out and should prepare in advance a list of questions. The interviewer should also be prepared for

My news, your news

Age range
Seven to eleven.

Media skill
Agency: children should learn to produce their own texts and be aware of the basic roles of reporter, editor, and paste-up artist.

Group size
Groups of four to six children, within a whole-class topic.

What you need
National and local newspapers, access to a typewriter or a computer with *Newspaper* software or a word-processing programme, photocopying or reprographic facilities.

some unexpected answers and be able to adapt to a new line of thought. Encourage questions that need more than just a yes or no answer.

Once the topics and questions have been prepared, the whole interview can be recorded on a portable tape recorder. The interviewer should stand or sit close to the person being interviewed, making her feel comfortable and at ease before the recording takes place. Have a warm-up session. Stress that good eye contact is important, as is listening to what the other person is saying.

After the interview, review the recording and decide how much will be used for writing up an article. This is a useful way of learning how to turn reported speech into prose. The children will realise that they can influence how someone or something is represented by their questioning and by their reporting.

What to do

The aim is to produce an interesting weekly newspaper. First ask the class to decide who will be the intended audience as this will govern what they write about and what viewpoints they project. Will it contain advertisements and illustrations? They will also need to work out how the finished news-sheet will be duplicated and circulated. Will there be a charge for the paper? Have a class production meeting to decide all the main points, features and jobs to be done.

Show the children some national and local papers and analyse the different types of text, such as reporting of news events, stories about people, sports, fashion, music, food, astrology, letters to the editor, editorial comments, etc. Explain to the children that reporters go out and research stories, then write them up as 'copy', which is given to the sub-editors, who check for spelling and accuracy and decide if the stories are right for the paper. Copy is then passed on to the editor, who makes the final selection.

Discuss with the class the many ways of filling a sheet of A4 paper. A newspaper has columns of a certain width and length, and the copy and pictures have to fit the space available. The copy should produce a pleasing balance and look good on the page. Some stories may warrant large type, important headlines and pictures alongside the text. Stories may need to be shuffled about and re-arranged.

Explain how some stories may need to be cut and how the editor must decide what should be left out. Other decisions must be made regarding the style and size of the type.

When the children have understood these processes, let them make their own class newspaper. Each child should be allocated a specific role within the production process. Get the class to work to a deadline so that the newspaper is finished by a pre-arranged time.

Let the children change roles each week so that they have experience of all aspects of newspaper production. If possible, exchange newspapers with another school.

The children will learn that newspaper production involves working co-operatively.

Past news

Age range
Seven to eleven.

Media skill
Technology: children should learn about the constraints and advantages of different equipment.

Group size
Groups of three or four children.

What you need
Access to libraries and museums, pencils, paper.

What to do
Find out how newspapers were produced in the past. How are they different today? Compare the old printing presses with today's desk-top publishing; hand-drawn illustrations with colour spread photographs. What about the use of facsimile machines and photocopiers? How many different ways can news reach people (oral, written, visual)? How does a story change according to the medium used? Is the story the same on radio, in a newspaper and on television?

Link this activity with other curriculum areas or project work in the class. Ask the children to write about a historical event in the form of a radio newsflash, television news or tabloid reporting. Topics could include the Gunpowder Plot, Joan of Arc, the execution of Mary, Queen of Scots or the signing of the Magna Carta.

Alternatively, ask them to enact a chat show and interview a famous historical character or have Shakespeare talk about one of his new plays.

The children will come to understand that technology has brought about greater freedom for reporting and faster transfer of information.

Talking heads

Age range
Seven to eleven.

Media skill
Language: children should discuss the features enabling them to recognise the different media forms, with special attention to the news on television.

Group size
Groups of six to eight children.

What you need
Video cassette recorder, pencils, paper, chair, table, stopwatch, clock, copies of photocopiable page 117.

What to do
Deconstruct a news broadcast by using a video tape that you can freeze frame and rewind. It is possible to rent specially made tapes for this purpose, which are copyright paid. The British Film Institute has a good selection of tapes accompanied by teachers' notes.

Look carefully at the way in which the sets are constructed. They are often quite simple, geometric in design, with the presenters sitting at a large conference-type

69

table, hiding their knees. Compare this with the relaxed set of a chat show, with easy chairs, coffee table and flowers in a vase. Why is this so? Look at the presenters' style of dress. Study the titles. What do the images such as pictures of the world and Big Ben suggest to you?

The news programme will have been put together very carefully to provide a balanced sequence. There will be opening and closing routines. Sometimes, the news reader will introduce the items as headlines, which are then dealt with more fully during the programme. The programme often finishes with a light-hearted item.

Divide the class into groups of six to eight children to form news production crews to plan, prepare and present a short news programme for a school assembly. The children should decide who will take on the different roles involved in research, reporting and writing.

The production team must see that everything is available and in place, and the director, like the editor on the newspaper, must make the choices and the decisions. You may also need an artist, a set designer and assistants to help everything run smoothly. Some children may be able to handle dual roles.

Be strict about working to a deadline and give the presentation a time limit of ten minutes. Start exactly on time with a countdown – 9,8,7,6 … . The news has to be up to the minute, so all the final arrangements will have to be made on the day. Make a list of the items to be included, plus the sequence and the timing of each item. Draw up a log, showing each item and its exact time, and what and who is needed (see photocopiable page 117). Have an item in reserve in case of mishap.

A script will need to be prepared showing the items to be included, interviews and visual material to be used, and the dialogue linking the items. Rehearse and check the timing, keeping a clock in view. Make sure the programme does not overrun. Decide whether you wish to give pre-publicity to the event and, if so, how this will be handled. You may also like to set up a viewers' feedback, with children from other classes writing down their comments about your presentation.

The children should be able to draw upon their perceptions of the conventions of news programmes in order to produce their own version. They will be aware of the way the newscaster sits and looks the viewer 'in the eye' and how interviews are conducted.

Communication

We communicate in a wide variety of forms and levels: intellectual, emotional and physical.

Sometimes a look can say a lot; a wave of the hand or a certain stance may be an intended signal and an unconscious body movement may reveal our innermost feelings.

When we enter a room we pick up a mass of information about the occupants before we even see them. The colours, furniture, books and paintings all help to communicate unspoken messages to us.

Media education helps children to be aware of all those visual and oral messages that have been constructed for a purpose. It also provides children with alternative ways of sending and receiving messages, allowing them to express their ideas, opinions and views of the world in forms other than the printed text.

The media is governed by a set of rules: there are certain codes and conventions, a language that needs to be learnt. Children can be helped to decode the language, to learn to read and understand and so become media-literate.

Media skills to be developed

Agency

This is one of the fundamental issues of media education. Who is communicating and why? What is the reason for this text? Children can be encouraged to find out the sources of production. They can become producers of their own work. They can investigate the number of reasons there are for communicating: personal, political, institutional, commercial and educational.

Categories

Children can find out the different ways of communicating: oral – one-to-one or to many – written, audio-visual, visual. A lot of work can be done investigating the special qualities that each media form offers.

Children can be encouraged to recognise and extend their knowledge through practical work. Poetry, dance, music and drama appeal to the intellect and emotions; news, documentaries and sport are more appropriate to interests and hobbies while soaps and comedy provide entertainment and diversion.

Media language

From a very early age children learn to understand their mothers' facial and body language; for example, they learn that a certain 'look' means 'behave' when they are misbehaving in public. In a similar way we learn to expect certain responses to stimuli, such as an ice cream van's jingle or the title sequence to *Neighbours*. Each medium has a message of its own, telling us what to expect.

Children are aware of media technology and they can recognise the devices used to express the passage of time such as, for example, pages falling from a calendar, misty focus to tell us it is all a dream, or cross-cutting from one scene to another.

Technology

What is the difference between using two tin cans and a piece of string to send a message and using a telephone answering machine? How many different ways can you copy a message? Is there a difference in quality, time, energy or cost?

Representation

Conjure up a visual image of a balloon. Think about what it represents – childhood laughter, parties, fun days, fairs. The reality is simple: a small inflated rubber sack secured to a string, yet it can give so much pleasure and evoke so many feelings and memories. Media texts depend on the audience's perception of the reality; if there is compatibility between text and reality, the text may be believable.

Audience

You may need to have someone with whom to communicate, but does your message get through to that person? How do people get their plays produced on television, or their books on to the shelves of W H Smith? How do you get people to look and listen? How big does your audience need to be?

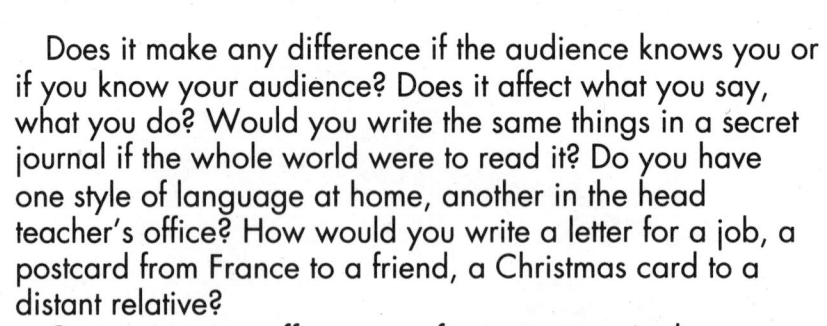

Does it make any difference if the audience knows you or if you know your audience? Does it affect what you say, what you do? Would you write the same things in a secret journal if the whole world were to read it? Do you have one style of language at home, another in the head teacher's office? How would you write a letter for a job, a postcard from France to a friend, a Christmas card to a distant relative?

Communication offers scope for interesting and exciting work across the curriculum, providing many chances for children to be involved in creative expression.

Is that really me?

Age range
Seven to nine.

Media skill
Representation: how does the media communicate its view of children? Is it how the children see themselves?

Group size
Whole class for discussion, then groups of six to eight children.

What you need
Children's books, magazines, scissors, comics, pencils, paper, scrap materials for making puppets.

What to do
Begin by looking at images of children in books. Try to find some pre-war story books or class readers as well as modern ones. Look closely at the hairstyles, clothing and activities. Look through magazine advertisements and cut out pictures of children. Do they correspond to the children in the class? How are they different? Talk about the programmes on children's television. Is *Grange Hill* a typical comprehensive school? What do the class think of the Saturday/Sunday morning programmes? Do they like the way the presenters run the show? Would they like more programmes such as *Why don't you?*

Discuss the portrayal of children in a current classic drama series. Can they identify with those children? Look at the images of children in comics. Is there any stereotyping? Ask the children to draw pictures of a studious child, the school sports hero, the class bully, a wimp and a tomboy.

Divide the class into groups and ask each group to develop a set of characters for a puppet play about life in a school. Let the groups decide what sort of school it is going to be: whether it is in a small village or a large town, whether it is multi-cultural, a boarding school, etc. Decide on the character types and what they will look like. Make a drawing and list five aspects of each character's personality. Draw up another list of personal details, such as age and family, in order to flesh out the character. Put together a script about an incident that takes place one morning at playtime. Make the puppets. Rehearse the play and perform it to the rest of the class.

Can the children analyse their findings and express their feelings about the way they are represented in the media? Can they draw on their own experiences to say how they see children?

Continue the idea of representation and look at the way other subjects are depicted. How are animals used in television advertisements? How are dragons and spiders shown? How are old people represented in soap operas, cartoons and advertisements? What message is coming across? Ask the children if the old people on television are like the old people that they know.

Postman Pat

Age range
Four to seven.

Media skill
Category: children should learn that they can be the communicators.

Group size
Small groups and individuals.

What you need
Stationery and office supplies, postman's outfit, trolley, pencils, paper, die, various letters.

What to do
Use a corner of the classroom as a post office and provide a wide variety of envelopes, postcards and parcel-making equipment. Ask the children to design their own stamps, letting them decide what they want to draw on them and their value. Let them use hole punches and rubber stamps. Provide plenty of paper so they can make and issue documents and licences. Try to provide a postman's uniform, with a cap and postbag, and a small trolley. Organise a postal service within the school.

Arrange a visit to the local post office or invite a postman into school to talk to the class about his work.

Ask the children to write to a favourite television personality or sportsman. Arrange for them to go to the post office to post their letters.

Let older children make a board game, using a die, following the route the postman takes to deliver his letters.

79

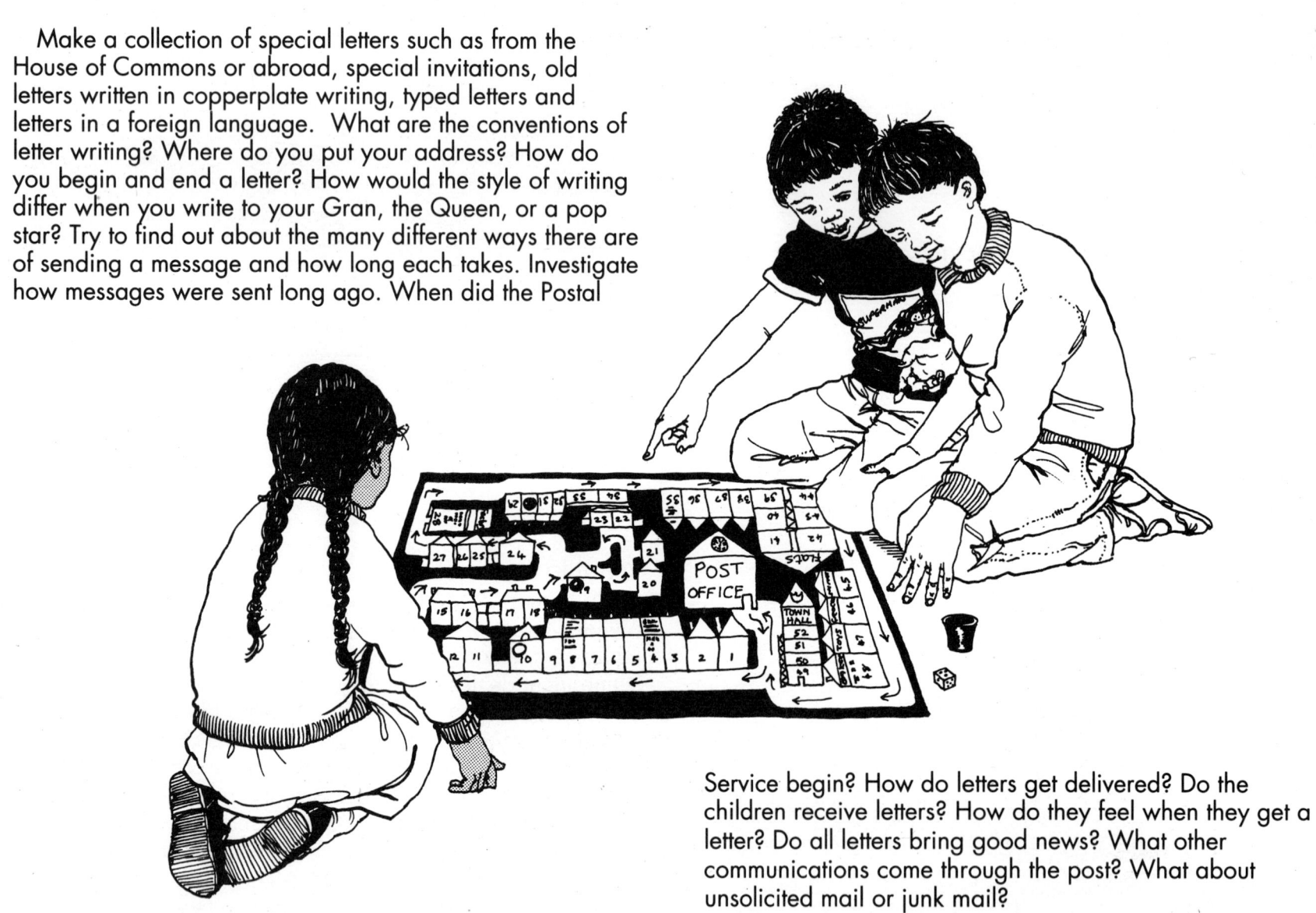

Make a collection of special letters such as from the House of Commons or abroad, special invitations, old letters written in copperplate writing, typed letters and letters in a foreign language. What are the conventions of letter writing? Where do you put your address? How do you begin and end a letter? How would the style of writing differ when you write to your Gran, the Queen, or a pop star? Try to find out about the many different ways there are of sending a message and how long each takes. Investigate how messages were sent long ago. When did the Postal Service begin? How do letters get delivered? Do the children receive letters? How do they feel when they get a letter? Do all letters bring good news? What other communications come through the post? What about unsolicited mail or junk mail?

Arrange for the children to exchange letters with a school in a different town or a different country. Send photographs and information about your locality as well as more personal material.

Is there anybody there?

Age range
Six to eight.

Media skill
Technology: what difference does the choice of equipment make to the meaning of a text?

Group size
Groups of three children.

What you need
Telephone directories, variety of containers, adhesive, scissors, wire, elastic bands, copies of photocopiable pages 118 and 119.

What to do
Discuss with the whole class how people have communicated in the past. Talk about the reasons for sending long-distance messages to people. Discuss various means of communication such as beacons, smoke signals, church bells, etc. Let the children learn some simple sentences in semaphore and Morse code (see photocopiable pages 118 and 119). Are all such messages about warning and danger, or are there other reasons for communicating?

Try to find out how and when the first telephones were invented. Investigate how a telephone works. Look for evidence of underground cables. Explore the system within the school by taking a group of children to a phone box and telephoning the school with a prepared message. Does the person on the other end interpret it correctly? Does she write it down or repeat it by word of mouth?

best? What is the furthest distance over which it works?

Are the children able to see the differences between the uses of the different equipment? Can they say which service is the most suitable? Would they send a letter if they wanted an answer within an hour? Would they use the telephone to send colour samples of furnishings?

Find out the costs of different communication services and compare them.

Try sending the same message in a variety of ways: semaphore, Morse code and other signals. How is it received or interpreted? Does the person receiving it need to have any special knowledge or instructions?

Discuss the telephone facilities, such as operator service, 999 calls and children's helpline. Let the children explore a telephone directory and find their own number if they have one.

Ask the groups to design an apparatus that will send messages across a distance. Which materials work the

Signs of the times

Age range
Five to seven.

Media skill
Language: the children should be able to observe and identify the signals all around them and the messages they convey.

Group size
Whole class divided into small working groups according to interest and ability.

What you need
A collection of signs and symbols, junk material and apparatus for CDT work, including bulbs, batteries and circuits, tape recorder, tapes providing sounds and music, art and craft supplies, copies of photocopiable page 120.

What to do
From birth children interpret signs and symbols. Pre-school children quickly learn messages through motivation, for example, the title music of their favourite television programme or an ice-cream van jingle. They can recognise a phone box, a police car, a school crossing. Some signs are obvious, others more obscure, requiring knowledge of the subject, or situation, to interpret their meaning.

Signals can be words, colours, lights, sounds and music. We know that while a red light usually means danger, a flashing light could be a warning, an advertisement or an invitation to participate in an entertainment.

Musical sound tracks prepare us for the mood or content of a programme. We can tell if it is going to be a comedy or a horror film.

Road signs are coded by shape to give information, warning or prohibition. What shapes are used?

Make a display of as many kinds of signs and symbols as you can find. Encourage the children to look out for them in their surroundings. Ask them to draw them and bring their drawings to school. Do they know the traffic light sequence? Take photographs of signs, then ask the children to say what they mean. Using photocopiable page 120, ask the children to identify the road signs and colour them in the appropriate colours.

Divide the class into groups of three and ask them to make some signs and signals for the school. Let them decide what they want to say and at whom the message is aimed. Where should the signs be positioned? What size and shape should they be? Should they give information or a warning? Should they advertise something or enforce a rule? What is the most effective medium? Do they involve sound, music, light, colour, pictures or symbols?

When the children have finished, and their signs or signals are in place, discuss how well each one works. Could they be improved? Are there any difficulties? Is the message understood?

Follow-up
Can the children identify correctly some of the signs from within their environment and from television programmes? Can they recognise music expressing specific emotions, such as suspense, sadness and happiness?

Explore in detail the 'mood' of different colours. Does a picture have the same effect if different colours are used? How can you express yourself in dance or mime? What feelings and emotions can be displayed without words?

Sensitivity

Age range
Four to seven.

Media skill
Audience: who receives a communication and what sense do they make of it?

Group size
Groups of about six children.

What you need
A collection of fabrics, card and scrap materials with a variety of textures, frieze paper, adhesive, blindfold, medium-sized box, a collection of small miscellaneous objects, scissors, card, tape recorder, tape, objects with a reflective surface, magnifying glasses, telephoto lens and binoculars, pin, copies of photocopiable page 121.

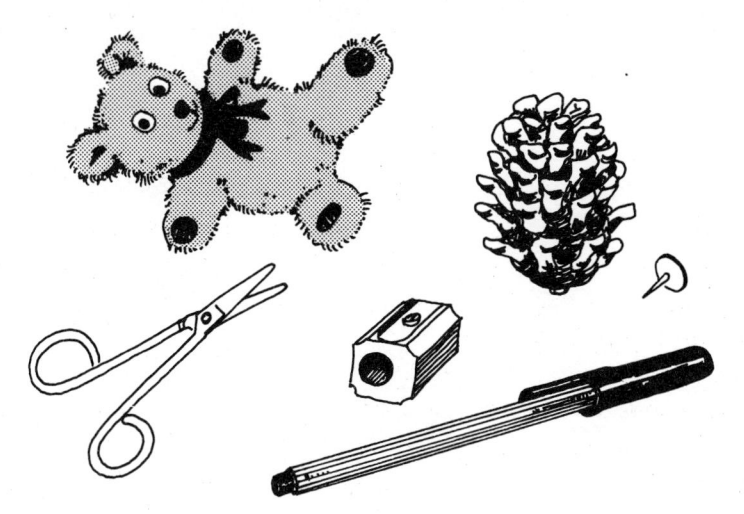

What to do

We receive communication through our senses. What happens if one or more of these senses does not function? Do messages alter or become confused? Do some messages need to be changed to help our understanding? Try the following activities to explore sensory awareness:

• Make a large 'feely wall' showing a scene from a well-known story. Have sections with obvious texture. Involve the children in the choice of textures. Are the colours important? Invite another class wearing blindfolds to come in and explore the picture. Ask them to describe what they think the picture is about. What are their reactions when they see it without the blindfolds?

• Put a varied selection of objects inside a 'feely box' (a box which allows the children to explore with their hands what is inside without being able to see the contents). Ask the children to guess what is there.

• Cut out some squares of differently textured fabric and stick them on to a piece of card. Cut out some identical squares, blindfold the children and ask them to match up the fabrics.

• Prepare a tape of everyday sounds and ask the children to identify them. Make another tape with more obscure sounds and compare the children's responses. Ask the children how near they have to be to hear particular sounds. Do some sounds carry better than others? Can the

children hear noises behind them? Do they hear better if they close their eyes? Can they tell a person's intentions through the sound of her voice? Do they need to see her face?
- Ask the children to write about what it is like on a foggy day, to be in the dark, or dazzled by bright lights. Ask them to shut one eye: what can they see? Is it exactly the same when they shut the other eye?
- Find reflections in a variety of surfaces such as mirrors, spoons, windows and silver paper. Do you get a true picture?
- How far away can you see? Look through a magnifying lens, telephoto lens and binoculars. What differences are there?
- Ask the children to talk about their experiences and their responses to stimuli. How do they think someone with a sensory malfunction would interpret the same stimuli?
- Using photocopiable page 121 for reference, ask the children to write a Braille message by pricking holes in a piece of card with a pin. Ask the children to try to read each other's messages.

Follow-up

The project could be the starting point for work on sight and optical illusion and could deal with zoetropes, flick books and animation. It could lead to investigation of how the eye works, animals' eyes and creatures without sight.

Other areas to follow up could include camouflage, change, sources of light and colour, shadows, transparency. This could be linked with work on photography (see the chapter on Production).

Non-verbal communication

Age range
Four to six.

Media skill
Language: the children will realise that communication does not necessarily have to be through words.

Group size
Groups of up to six children for role play with whole class involvement.

What you need
Old clothes for dressing up, tape recorder or record player, recordings of atmospheric music.

What to do
Children learn to interpret non-verbal communication from birth almost unconsciously. Use the following ideas with younger children to encourage an awareness of non-verbal communication:
- Ask a group of children to mime a situation with which they are all familiar such as a parent telling a child that it is time to go to bed or a child returning from school and

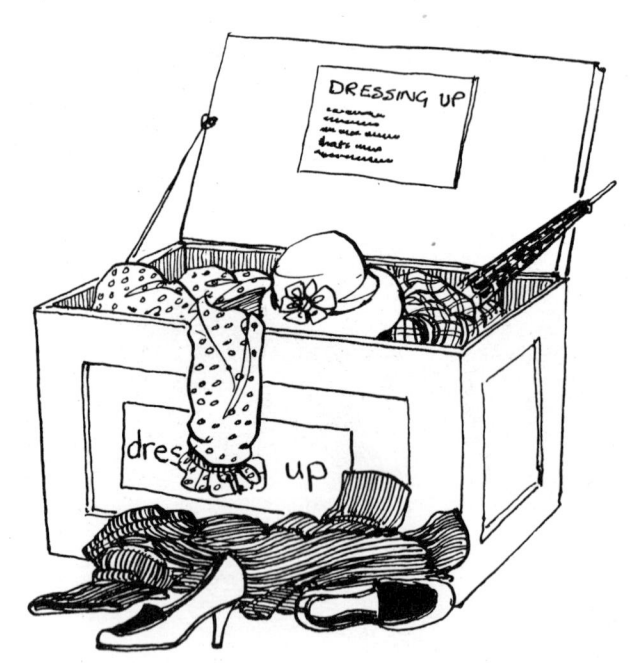

seeing their pet dog. Stress that they should not use any words.
- Collect together various articles of old clothing, hats, masks etc, for dressing up. Let the children dress up and ask them to guess what they are each trying to be.
- Record a selection of different kinds of instrumental music and ask the children what they think the music is meant to represent. Good atmospheric pieces include Saint-Saens' *Carnival of the Animals*, Beethoven's *Pastoral Symphony*, Mendelssohn's *Fingal's Cave*, Ibert's *Escales* and Vaughan Williams' *The Lark Ascending*. Ask them to explain their interpretations of the music.

Production

One of the most exciting aspects of media work is when children take charge of their own productions. They learn very quickly when allowed to use technical equipment by themselves. By being involved in a production the children will actively employ media concepts. They will need to plan well, taking into account the constraints of time and the cost of materials. They will need to decide upon the most suitable medium, who their audience will be and how to reach them. They will be working collaboratively as a team.

Media skills to be developed

Agency
By being in charge of the production the children become the agency, the ones who make the decisions and the choices as to how the finished product will be. They will begin to feel the constraints and the responsibility.

Categories
The children will need to decide how they will present their production – will it be a documentary, a news item, a drama? Will it be film, video, drawn animation or 3D? To be able to make a choice it is necessary to be aware of and be able to recognise the genre or style.

Media language
Children draw upon their knowledge of the media and recreate the formats they are familiar with, the style of presenting, interviewing techniques, titles and credits.

Technology
The children learn best through 'hands on' experience, and will need to decide how and where the equipment will be placed. They may decide to use special effects, stop frame, diffusers, unusual angles or lighting to improve their production.

Representation
As the producers, they will need to decide how to represent their subject. Can it be shown in different ways or from different viewpoints; it is a biased or one sided view? How do you give a true picture? Does it always have to be a real life situation? What about fantasy? Is there any stereotyping in the make-believe world?

Audience
They will need to consider who their audience will be. Does it make a difference if you know you audience? Does it affect what you might put into the media text? How can you decide what their reactions might be?

Pinhole camera

Age range
Seven to eleven.

Media skill
Making a pinhole camera and developing the photograph.

Group size
Pairs or individuals.

What you need
Biscuit tin with tight-fitting lid, non-reflective black paint, paintbrush, bradawl, black insulating tape, photographic paper, scissors, adhesive tape, darkroom with orange or red safelight, four developing trays, developer, fixer, water, tongs, sheet of glass or perspex.

What to do
Paint the inside and lid of a biscuit tin with non-reflective black paint. Use a bradawl to make a small neat hole in the tin (Figure 1). Cover the hole with black insulating tape.

Figure 1

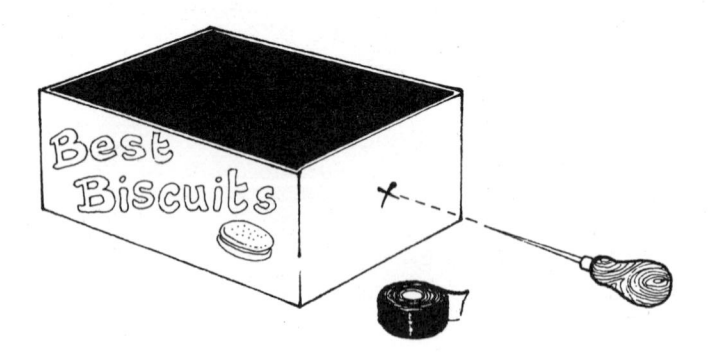

You can use any store cupboard as a darkroom, provided all light is blocked out, and there is a shelf on which to stand the developing trays, as well as a safelight and a lamp for making positive prints.

Load the film in the darkroom with the safelight on. Cut a notch along the top edge of the photographic paper to help identify it later. Use adhesive tape to fix the paper inside

Figure 2

the tin, opposite the hole (Figure 2). Put the lid on the tin and secure it well with black insulating tape. The camera is now ready to use.

To take pictures, the camera needs to be firm and steady, so position it carefully, then remove the tape covering the pinhole.

The exposure times will vary depending on the size of the hole, the brightness of the day and the distance from the hole to the paper. On a bright day you may only need half a minute, but on a dull day it could be much longer. It will probably take several attempts to get it right, so try not to let the children become discouraged if they do not succeed straight away. Replace the insulating tape over the hole immediately after each exposure.

In the darkroom, prepare four trays, one containing developer, another fixer and two, water. Switch on the safelight, open the tin and remove the paper. Place the paper in the tray of developer until a negative image appears. If it goes completely black it was exposed for too long. Wash the paper in a tray of water for a couple of minutes. Next, put the paper into the tray of fixer for approximately four minutes and wash it in the second tray of water. It can now be dried. The image will be upside down.

Encourage the use of tongs as some children may have an allergic reaction to the chemicals. Also the chemicals will not work efficiently if they are mixed.

Make a positive print by taking a fresh piece of photographic paper and laying the negative face down on to it. Hold it flat with the piece of glass. Shine a light on to it for a moment: an eight watt bulb works well, giving a good contrast. Repeat the printing steps. The chemicals can be bottled and stored for future use.

This experience is completely different from the point-and-shoot photography of a purchased camera. The concept of focal length and reversed image can be explained and demonstrated, and the idea of exposure time easily grasped. The children will find it very exciting to watch their own pictures appear.

Over- or under-exposed prints can be used as a game, where the children guess what the mystery object is, or even as a stimulus for creative writing.

Follow-up
Ask the children to write about what they have done. Can they draw the project in sequence?

Let the children design and construct their own framework for a camera using 1cm squared pine, joining the corners with cardboard triangles to form cubes of varying sizes. The sides should be well sealed, with one side hinged for access. The different sizes will produce different focal lengths.

Further work could be undertaken to explore light transmission, positive and negative images, wide angle and telephoto lenses.

Photography

Age range
Seven to nine.

Media skill
Using a camera. Making decisions about choice of shot and arrangement within the frames.

Group size
Small groups and individuals.

What you need
A collection of old cameras, a camera for the children to use, black-and-white and colour film, tripod, sticky labels.

What to do
Allow the children to examine some old cameras, framing shots through the viewfinder and drawing what they can see. Let them investigate the mechanisms.

Invite someone from a local amateur photographic society to talk to the children about photography and to show them examples of her work.

Let the children handle the camera they are going to use. Read the instructions through together. Colour code the parts of the camera with sticky labels to link with the relevant instructions.

Let the children take some photographs for themselves, but be at hand to give advice. It must be the children's work, their eyes behind the lens, their hand on the button. Encourage them to keep a photo log with names, dates, places and name of the person who took the photograph. This can be transferred as a caption once the photograph has been developed. Keeping a log also helps with the review discussion later on.

Encourage the children to plan the shots and make a sketch of what they think will be in them. Use the photographs in different ways:
- Photographs can be mounted and used as work cards.
- Make a map of the environment, using photos to highlight areas.
- Use photographs of school events and sell them for fund-raising.
- Record changes, such as the growth of a plant or the development of a building site.
- Let the children keep a photographic record of work they have done, for example, a model, a construction or a painting.

- Use photographs to freeze action or make things appear larger. Use these facilities to study mini-beasts.
- Compare colour and black-and-white pictures of the same subject.
- Use photographs to construct a narrative. Let the children use between six and eight photographs to tell a visual story.
- Experiment with cropping or enlarging photographs, using them for collage, mixed with other media.
- Poorly focused, blurred pictures can be used for imaginative story-making.

The children will begin to handle the camera confidently as a tool after they have had the experience of using it. They will be more selective and more accurate. They will begin to examine other photographs with a more critical eye.

Follow-up

Cameras can be used to explore the world outside school. Compare old photographs with ones the children have taken to show how the town or village has changed.

Use photographs in mathematical work, looking for shapes and patterns, the symmetry of a building or climbing apparatus.

Photograph things from unusual angles and viewpoints.

Help younger children understand the structure of school life by building up a photographic record of the school day, week or year.

Photographs can be used as the starting point for art and craft, with the subject represented later in clay, needlework and fabric.

Tape/slide

Age range
Seven to eleven.

Media skill
Children should be able to produce a simple visual narrative and match it with a sound-track.

Group size
Individuals or small groups.

What you need
Acetate film, OHP (overhead projector) pens, pieces of coloured film, photographic negatives, paint, glassless slide mounts, tape recorder, tapes, slide projector.

What to do
Let the children draw directly on to pieces of acetate with the OHP pens. The drawings can be abstract or representational. Cut out and mount the acetate into the frames and let the children project their drawings on to a screen. Let them experiment by projecting on to walls, bodies and fabric or by mixing two or more projections together. Let the children try sandwiching translucent materials, old negatives or blobs of paint between the slides. Experiment and explore.

The children can construct a sequence to communicate a message or provide a background for dance and drama work.

Explore the differences in narrative by changing the running order of the slides. Which sequence is the most effective? Why? What happens when you take out some of the pictures or change their position?

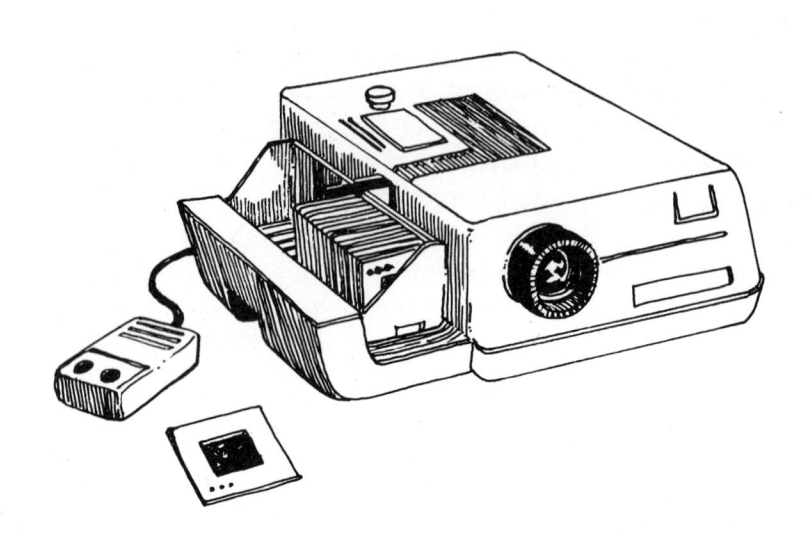

Ask the children to record their own music or sound-track to accompany the images, or let them illustrate a favourite piece of music. They could write a script and do a voice-over. Try using different types of sounds. Do they make any difference to the understanding of the production?

The children should understand how sounds and images can be edited to produce different meanings. They should be able to work the projector and obtain a clear well-focused image.

Follow-up
The children could produce their own slide photographs using black-and-white or colour film.

They could produce more ambitious sound effects, with a portastudio and several projectors allowing dissolves and fades.

Storyboard

Age range
Six to eight.

Media skill
Children should be able to plan a simple narrative structure using visual techniques.

Group size
Groups of six to eight children or individuals.

What you need
Large sheets of paper, ruler, pencils.

What to do
When you decide to make a visual production such as an animated film, a video, or a tape/slide show, it is necessary to know what you want to say and to whom, how you are going to say it, what medium you will use, how much time is available and what angle or viewpoint you will take.

The group will need to plan it out beforehand and discuss all the details. This usually takes the form of a visual script, or storyboard, with the story told in a series of pictures that highlight the main points and break the story down into the important elements (Figure 1).

Get the children to mark out large squares on a sheet of paper, with a space for comments beneath each square. Draw a picture in each square to show the action for each scene and to illustrate the development of the story. Show either a magnified detail of a scene to emphasise a point or a general view to set the mood. The children can use more than one picture to give the same information. There is no right or wrong way as long as the audience understands the message.

Which is the most effective method and gives the clearest information? Sometimes it will be necessary to restrict the length of a production. Discuss the scenes with the group: is this picture really necessary to the story, does it add something special or can we do without it? Ask the groups to give indications of timing and the soundtrack for each scene. Try sequencing a set of eight pictures to tell the same story in different ways; as a thriller or a comedy with a

Figure 1

Tape recorders

Age range
Five to seven.

Media skill
Children should be able to operate simple equipment and make decisions about when to use it.

Group size
Individuals and small groups.

What you need
Tape recorder, tapes, microphones, headphones, percussion instruments.

What to do
Many children will already be familiar with tape recorders; nevertheless, show them how to use them, read the

happy ending. Look at comic books to see how they use close-ups and cut-aways to let you know what is happening elsewhere. Give the children a set of characters and a location, then let them draw their different ideas for a story.

A storyboard can be an abstract collection of shapes and images, that changes, reforms and makes patterns. You do not need to draw really well; stick figures are adequate and will serve just as well.

The children should be able to plan and prepare a sequence of images to tell a simple story. Is the meaning clear?

Follow-up
Prepare a storyboard and use it for an animation project (see Animation, page 103).

instructions together and introduce a colour code for stop, play and rewind. Let the children devise their own symbols and signs. Keep the cassettes in tidy boxes, clearly labelled and catalogued. If possible, keep an area of the class screened off, where the children can use headphones and make recordings. Listening activities stimulate the imagination.

Tape record stories for the children to listen to. Let them listen to them over and over again if they wish. Record a selection of sounds for the children to identify and match with pictures. Record a set of instructions (eg stand on one leg, clap your hands, curl up on the floor), play the tape to the children and ask them to carry out the instructions.

Record a sequence of rhythms and ask the children to repeat them with percussion instruments.

Serialise stories on tape. Record sounds or music and ask the children to paint what they hear (these could later form part of a slide/tape show).

Let the children record their own stories. Can they identify each other's voices from the recordings?

Let the children record interviews with each other about what they have been doing that day. Let them interview the caretaker, the dinner ladies, the school secretary. Ask them to prepare their questions in advance.

Follow-up
Use a tape recorder as a production tool, incorporating it into making a video, film or tape/slide presentation. Learn how to edit tapes, looking at reel-to-reel tape recorders and Uhers. Experiment with portastudios and multiple soundtracks.

Let the children use the tape recorder as a way of recording their news, their comments and findings about their work.

Let the children listen to the recordings in small groups. Allow members to make constructive criticism, ie they can make a comment to improve the work, but not to say 'that's rubbish'. Discuss different ways of improving the recordings, and making them clearer and more interesting. What is the best way of speaking into a microphone?

The children should become confident in their use of a tape recorder.

Animation

Animation means, literally, bringing to life. Technically, it is the creation of an illusion of movement. It is a strange mixture of art, craft, design and technical know-how.

It can be used in education across the curriculum, as a tool for media work, in community programmes and for advertising and promotions. It is an alternative to print as a means of exchanging ideas and communication.

It is a relatively inexpensive form of film-making, especially suitable for younger children. It can involve the whole class.

It can be a rewarding and enjoyable experience.

Animation without a camera

Age range
Seven to eleven.

Media skill
Producing a media text.

Group size
Groups of any size or individuals.

What you need
Exposed or clear leader film (16mm or 35mm), a piece of flat wood slightly wider than the film, two thin strips of card the same length as the wood, adhesive, tacks or pins, hammer, white card, scissors, pencil, OHP (overhead projector) pens, selection of sharp instruments, splicing machine, projector.

What to do
Before starting your animation, try to show the children some examples of Len Lye's work, from the National Film Board of Canada, which demonstrates the use of line and colour.

Make a holding block, which is a piece of wood that holds the film steady while the animator draws on it. The piece of wood should be slightly wider than the width of the film and long enough to take at least 24 frames. Stick the two long thin strips of card along the sides of the length of wood so that a channel is formed in which the film can sit (Figure 1).

Figure 1

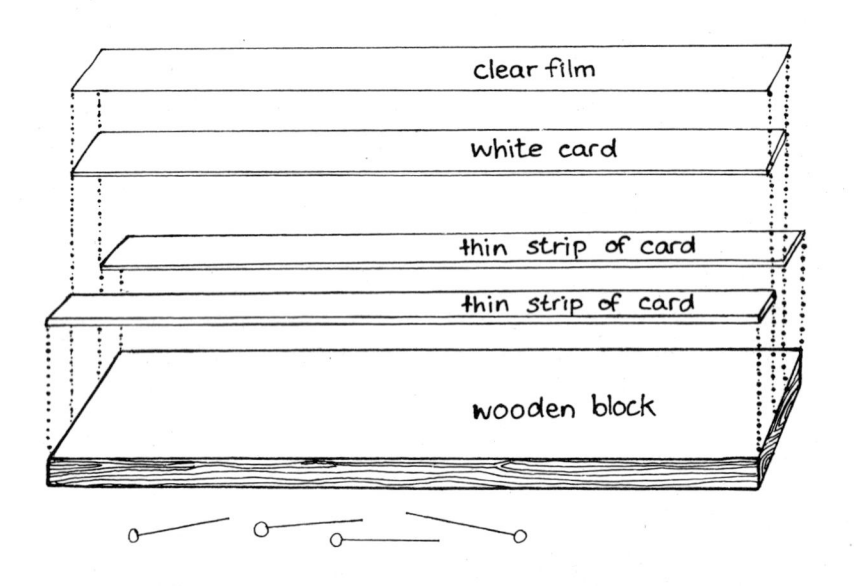

- clear film
- white card
- thin strip of card
- thin strip of card
- wooden block

Hammer in some tacks or pins on each side of the block at one end. Secure the film by slipping the sprocket holes of the film over the tacks (Figure 2).

Cut a strip of white card so that it fits inside the holding block. Mark on the card the correct frame lines for the size of the film. Draw the intended animation sequence on to the white card strip, frame by frame, then lay it in the holding block and place the clear leader film on top, fixing it to the tacks. Encourage abstract, rather than representational, designs.

Trace the design frame by frame. Continue until the sequence is finished. The film can now be run through a projector and viewed straight away. A soundtrack will add to the impact.

Figure 2

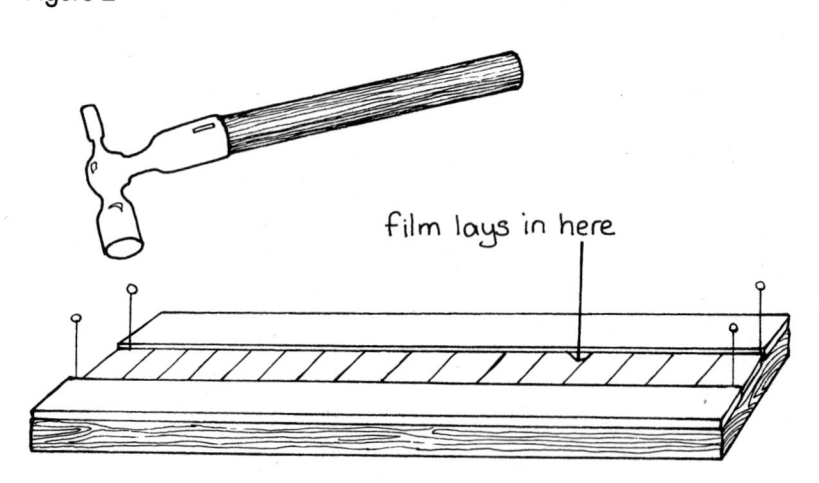

film lays in here

A whole class can work on a roll of film in this way. The film can be cut into long strips and joined later. Let each child be responsible for three to five seconds of animation, ie between 72 and 120 individual frames. Film can be joined using either adhesive tape or film cement with a splicing machine. If possible provide cotton gloves for the children to wear when handling the film to avoid greasy marks on the emulsion.

Alternatively, try working on fogged film, which is black, so you cannot see the frame lines. Work on the dull side, the emulsion. Scratch away the emulsion with fine pointed instruments. This allows the projector light to shine through, making a black-and-white image. Be sure to get rid of the scrapings as they could clog up the projector.

The children should soon grasp the principle of persistence of vision.

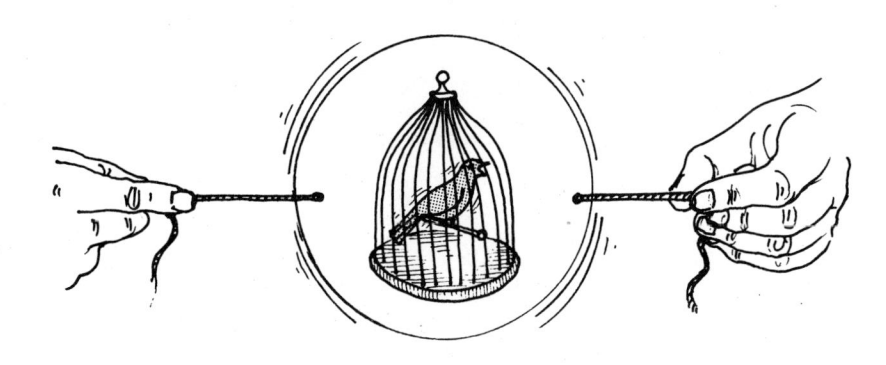

Follow-up
Experiment with making flick books and optical illusion toys. Investigate magnification and projection. Look at positive and negative images.

Animation with a camera

Age range
Six plus.

Media skill
To be able to make representations in a media text.

Group size
Whole class, with a working group of four to six children.

What you need
Variety of craft materials for making models, Super-8 cine camera with single frame facility and cable release, tripod, two 200 watt lights, a strong table, film, cine projector, tape recorder, tape, copies of photocopiable pages 122 and 123.

What to do
Explain the concept of animation to the children and discuss the medium which you will use. Try to keep the medium simple, as the purpose of the activity is for the

children to learn about technique and timing. Animation can be done using a wide variety of media:
- Drawings, representational or abstract.
- Cut-outs, montage, photos, pictures or a combination of these.
- Three-dimensional models made from toys, modelling clay, or objects such as leaves, fruit, feathers, etc.
- Substances such as sand, rice and spaghetti, cut-outs on a light box (a box with the top made of opaque glass with lights shining through from underneath so that the objects become silhouettes).

Explain that animation is an illusion. It is necessary to move the objects – or make different drawings – several times for one second of real time on the screen. Your camera will shoot at either 18 frames or 24 frames. Check to see which. This means that 18 or 24 frames of film (depending on the camera) will pass through the projector gate for each second of real time. To make realistic movement on the screen, take two frames, move the object approximately 1cm, take another two frames, and move again.

When making models for animation, take into consideration the fact that parts of the model may need to be moved frequently and could fall off. Anything that does not need to move should be firmly stuck down. It is easy to knock the table and give the appearance of an earthquake! Never remove anything from the set without previously marking its place, as it is almost impossible to replace it exactly.

The technique of animation can be used to illustrate a

story, show movements on a map, demonstrate an experiment, or create movement to music. The list is endless. The children can control the set. It is only when the cable release is pressed that the camera takes the shot, so there is no pressure on them to hurry.

The children should be clear about what they are aiming for and think about the intended audience. Discuss and plan the storyboard, drawing the sequence of events. Arrange the shooting programme in sequence. Do not forget the titles and credits.

It is best if everyone in the group participates in making backgrounds and characters. Prepare the artwork, backgrounds and models. Rehearse the moves before you film, check if any characters need to enter from the other side of the set, as you will need a duplicate but facing in the opposite direction. Will the film be two-dimensional (Figure 1) or three-dimensional (Figure 2)?

Figure 1

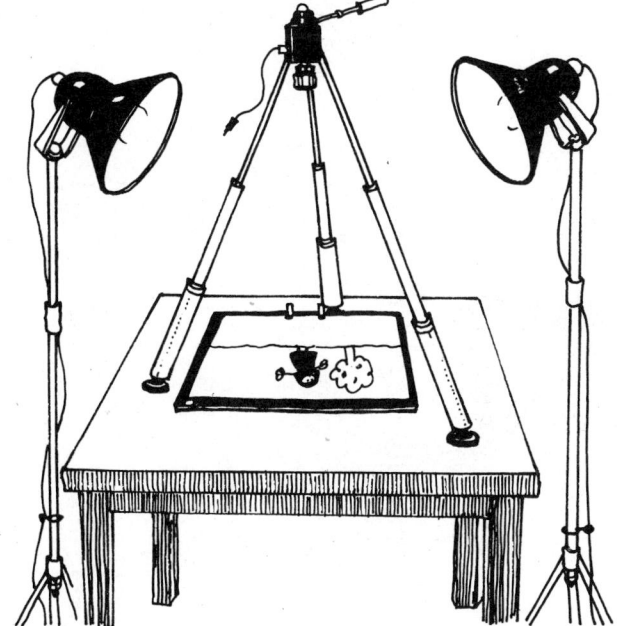

Figure 2

When you are ready to start filming you will need someone on the camera to press the cable release, someone to keep a tally of the shots and to make sure everyone's hands are off the set before the shot is taken, and the rest of the group to move the characters on the set. Keep a shooting log using photocopiable pages 122 and 123. The children can rotate the jobs so that they have a go at each one.

Make sure the children observe the following points when filming:
- Check the field of view and mark the perimeters. Have a piece of card fixed on the area where you are going to film. Look through the viewfinder, adjust the focus. Mark the top, bottom and sides of the paper so you know exactly what space you have to work within.
- Adjust focus and distance. Place some black-on-white print on the area and adjust the focus until the print is sharp and clear.

- Check the light meter is not in the red.
- If using a tripod, make sure it is firm and safe. Remember to switch on the camera and switch off after filming.
- Keep a spare supply of batteries and lights.

Do not be afraid to let the children experiment. Often the best ideas come once they are familiar with the process.

The film will have to be sent away for processing. This takes about two weeks, which needs to be considered when planning a date for showing the production. Add a soundtrack on its return.

View the film and ask the children if they would change anything. How would they improve it? Make another film using a different technique.

There are many examples of excellence in production, artwork and narrative. Try to view some of the Masters of Animation films, which can be loaned from the British Film Institute or the National Film Board of Canada.

Video

Video cameras are becoming increasingly accessible and provide children with active involvement and hands-on experience. Making a video involves the whole range of media-education concepts and skills. It helps to demystify broadcast productions and separates the image from reality. It will give them understanding of the process and make them more critical consumers.

Age range
Seven plus.

Media skills
Video production involves all areas of media skills.

Agency: the children are the ones who make the decisions. They work as part of a team, interacting and involved in the whole production. They work to a deadline, find locations, arrange interviews and sort out the problems.

Categories: the children have to decide what form their work will take and what will be the style and genre. To do this they must be able to recognise the different categories.

Technique: they will have to choose what will be the 'look' of the finished video, the structure and the balance of the scenes, titles, frames and cutaways. How many cameras will they use? Where will they be situated?

Audience: they will have to be able to see things from other people's points of view, make judgements as to presentation and how it should be received.

Language and conventions: the children will need to recognise their own perceptions, why certain seating arrangements indicate a formal discussion, how fast cutting and editing set the pace and when to use a close-up. They should learn what is meant by mix shots, close-up, long shot, pan and fade in/out.

Representation: they will need to understand that the same object can be shown in different ways and can produce different responses. How will they choose to represent their subject? Why?

Group size
The whole class can be involved in planning and preparing, but it is best to keep the camera crew to three: camera, sound, director.

What you need
A video camera or camcorder with tape and batteries, tripod, a separate microphone fixed to an extension handle, the use of two video recorders for rough editing.

What to do
Do not try to film the whole school play, the entire sports day or leavers' assembly. However, you can make ten minutes of edited highlights, cut with interviews and background information, that will be entertaining to watch

and a very useful exercise for the children. Video makers can be very self-indulgent, so remind the children that audiences become bored quickly. Other ideas are:
- Make an advertisement of 25 to 30 seconds duration.
- Write part of a soap opera and get each group to take turns continuing the story from where it left off.
- Young children can film a series of paintings to tell a story.
- Film objects from unusual angles, or make a quiz game by slowly bringing objects into focus and letting the children guess what they are.

- Make memory recall games by filming a sequence of events.
- Take the camera on field trips to record special features. Use the macro facility to magnify objects, and in the classroom, use the freeze frame for close observational work.
- Plan and produce a simple maths programme for another class.
- Make a treasure trail to be followed up outdoors.

Let the children explore what the camera can do. Let them learn about its facilities and how to use them. The end results are important but do not be disappointed if you do not get broadcast quality: that costs thousands of pounds. The process is what matters.

Production team

There are various jobs to choose from.
- Artwork and graphics: this includes titles and credits, words, pictures, models, promotion, advertising and tickets.
- Lighting: most cameras will operate in poor lighting conditions, but you may wish to have special effects or use lighting to highlight certain areas.
- Sounds: decide if there are to be any special sound effects or any pre-recorded sections. The microphone is best used attached to a broom handle, with a crew member holding it close to the person who is talking. Watch out that the microphone does not pick up unwanted sound.
- Scripts: this includes the storyboard and words, introductions, links, recaps, conclusions, wind-ups and thank-yous. The crew need to know what is happening, when and where. Dialogue should be scripted, rehearsed and timed.
- Sets and props: sets may need to be designed and arranged. Gather together all materials and equipment. Make sure the set looks good and that everything is at hand in the right place. Ensure continuity and make a list for each scene. Pack away at the end, after shooting.
- Camera crew: an assistant to keep a log of the shots, a director, who decides the shots and position of the camera and makes the decisions, and, of course, the camera operator. When filming, fix the camera on a tripod to ensure steady shots.

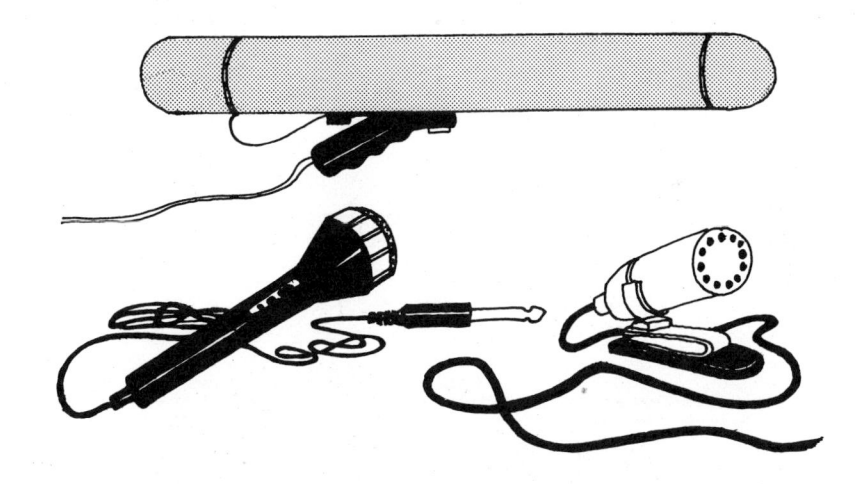

Review your video. Could you have improved upon it? How did you use the end product? Would you make another one?

Does the finished video allow you to understand how television works?

Reproducible material

Ads, ads everywhere, see page 28

SHOPPING SURVEY

What has been purchased?

Food ☐

Beverages ☐

Toiletries ☐

Domestic utensils/cleaning materials ☐

Stationery/newspapers/magazines ☐

Other

Do you buy the shop's own brand goods? Do you think they are as good as other brands?

What makes you choose a particular brand of goods?

Does the way an article is packaged affect your choice?

Would you buy goods that were not decoratively packaged?

What do you like or dislike about the way items are packaged?

Do you think manufacturers put too much packaging on goods?

This page may be photocopied for use in the classroom and should not be declared in any return in respect of any photocopying licence.

How do we watch? See page 48

QUESTIONNAIRE ONE: VIEWING HABITS

How old are you?

Do you have any brothers or sisters? If so, how many?

Do you have a television at home?

Is it black and white or colour?

How much television do you watch in one day?

Do you have a video?

Do you watch television at weekends?

What else do you do in your free time?

Who decides what programmes you will watch?

Do you watch advertisements? Which ones are your favourites?

Do you have any toys or books relating to television programmes? If so, what?

This page may be photocopied for use in the classroom and should not be declared in any return in respect of any photocopying licence.

How do we watch? See page 48

QUESTIONNAIRE TWO – FAVOURITE PROGRAMMES

What kind of programmes do you like? Please tick.

☐ Magazine programmes (eg *Blue Peter*)
☐ Cartoons (eg *Bugs Bunny*)
☐ Quiz programmes
☐ Films
☐ Adventures
☐ Serials
☐ Soap operas (eg *Neighbours*)
☐ Comedies
☐ Nature
☐ Documentaries
☐ Music (eg *Top of the Pops*)
☐ Sport
☐ Other _____

This page may be photocopied for use in the classroom and should not be declared in any return in respect of any photocopying licence.

How do we watch? see page 48

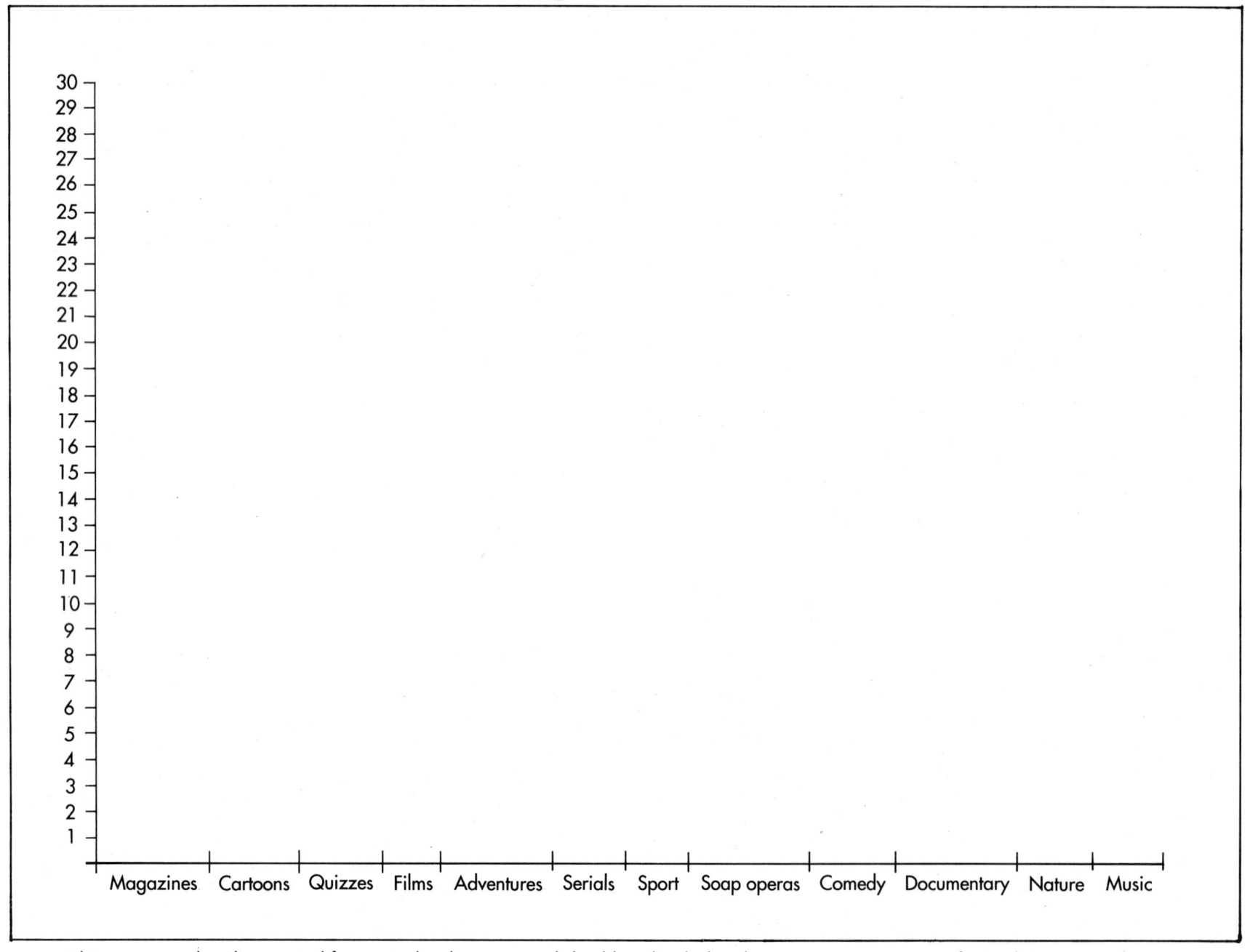

30
29
28
27
26
25
24
23
22
21
20
19
18
17
16
15
14
13
12
11
10
9
8
7
6
5
4
3
2
1

Magazines Cartoons Quizzes Films Adventures Serials Sport Soap operas Comedy Documentary Nature Music

This page may be photocopied for use in the classroom and should not be declared in any return in respect of any photocopying licence.

Talking heads, see page 69

	ITEM	PRESENTER	DURATION	WHAT YOU NEED
1				
2				
3				
4				
5				
6				

This page may be photocopied for use in the classroom and should not be declared in any return in respect of any photocopying licence.

Is there anybody there? see page 81

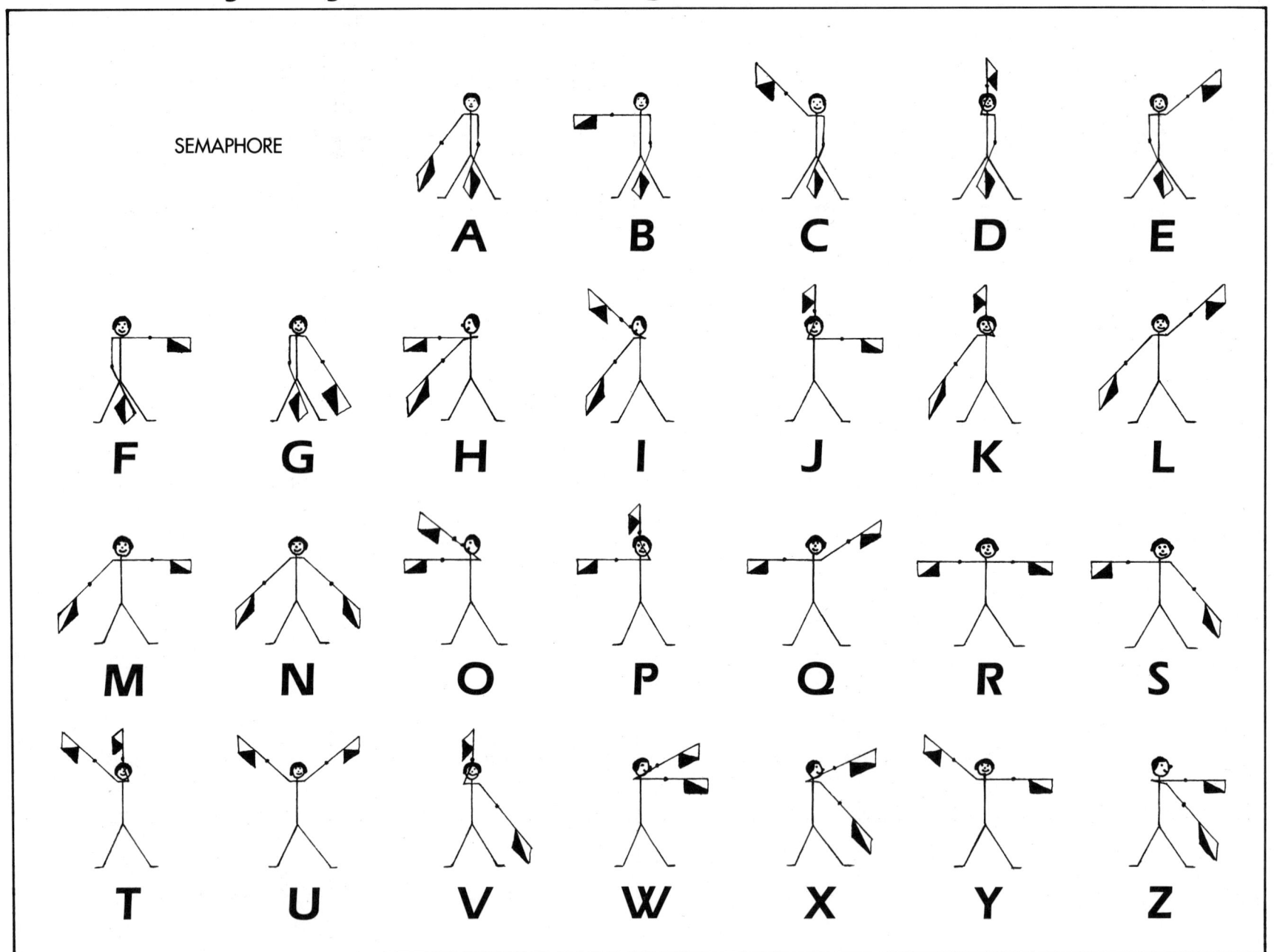

SEMAPHORE

A B C D E
F G H I J K L
M N O P Q R S
T U V W X Y Z

This page may be photocopied for use in the classroom and should not be declared in any return in respect of any photocopying licence.

Is there anybody there? see page 81

MORSE CODE		M − −	T −
A · −	G − − ·	N − ·	U · · −
B − · · ·	H · · · ·	O − − −	V · · · −
C − · − ·	I · ·	P · − − ·	W · − −
D − · ·	J · − − −	Q − − · −	X − · · −
E ·	K − · −	R · − ·	Y − · − −
F · · − ·	L · − · ·	S · · ·	Z − − · ·

This page may be photocopied for use in the classroom and should not be declared in any return in respect of any photocopying licence.

Signs of the times, see page 83

ROAD SIGNS

Colour the signs in the appropriate colours and write underneath what you think they mean.

Sensitivity, see page 85

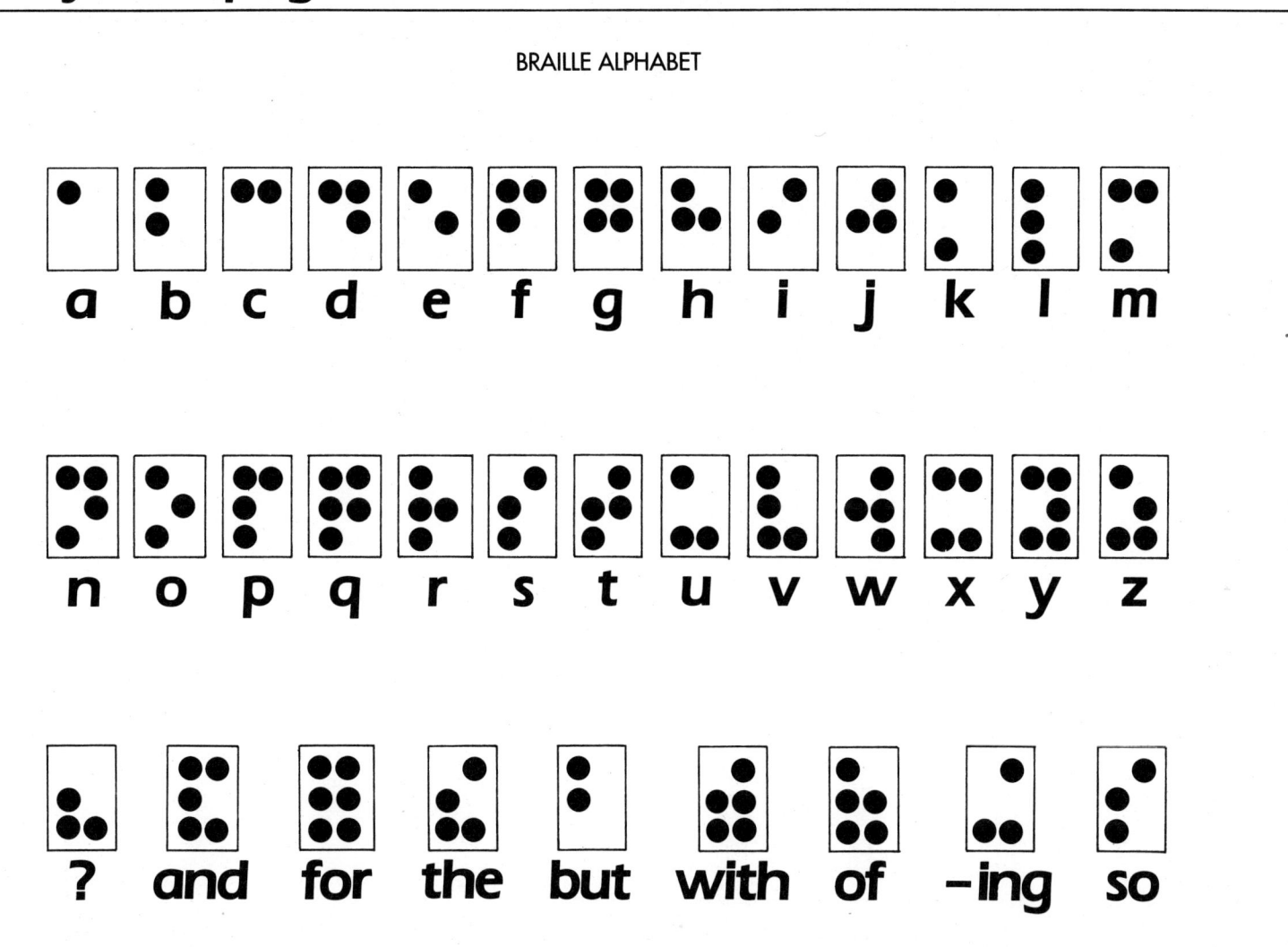

BRAILLE ALPHABET

a b c d e f g h i j k l m

n o p q r s t u v w x y z

? and for the but with of -ing so

This page may be photocopied for use in the classroom and should not be declared in any return in respect of any photocopying licence.

Animation with a camera, see page 105

SHOOTING LOG 18 frames per second 2 frames per shot	TIME									1 SEC									2 SEC
	SOUND																		
	ACTION																		
	SCENE																		
	FRAME NOS	1.2	3.4	5.6	7.8	9.10	11.12	13.14	15.16	17.18	19.20	21.22	23.24	25.26	27.28	29.30	31.32	33.34	35.36

This page may be photocopied for use in the classroom and should not be declared in any return in respect of any photocopying licence.

Animation with a camera, see page 105

SHOOTING LOG (Photocopy and fill in numbers as required.)

TIME																				
SOUND																				
ACTION																				
SCENE																				
FRAME NOS																				

This page may be photocopied for use in the classroom and should not be declared in any return in respect of any photocopying licence.

Glossary

Audience Anyone who receives a text, whether an audience of thousands attending a concert or an audience of one person reading a book or watching television.

AVA Audio visual aids such as tape recorders, slide projectors, cameras, film and television.

Camcorder A portable video camera.

Code The devices used to help the viewer recognise what sort of programme it is. The sets, the presenters and style of a news programme, quiz show or documentary help the viewer interpret the message.

Conventions Strategies for conveying meaning. For example, we recognise that books with large print and colourful illustrations are intended for younger readers and that someone on television who is smartly dressed and seated behind a desk surrounded by a simple set is likely to be a newsreader.

Cut Changing from one scene in a film to another.

Deconstruct To analyse a programme, investigating how the images have been constructed.

Dissolve An image being mixed into the next.

Documentary A programme that deals with current issues and real life events.

Fade To change scenes in a film by fading a picture to black or from black to another picture.

Focal length The distance between the camera and the subject.

Focus The point at which the subject of a film is well defined and clear.

Frame The limits as seen through the camera lens. In animation films are made frame by frame, one picture at a time.

Genre Classification of a media text by type, eg science fiction, comedy, nostalgic.

Lith film Black and white film used for graphics work.

Location The place where filming takes place.

Log A record of the film work: the location, the props, the type of shot etc.

Macro A camera lens that allows the user to film very close to the subject.

Portastudio Portable electronic keyboard, offering a variety of different sounds and rhythms.

Script The written record of a programme, play or film. It tells everyone involved in the production what to do. In an animated film this is often in a visual form such as a series of pictures.

Sit com A situation comedy, often a series of programmes with a comedy slant.

Soap opera A never-ending story where the characters' lives are interwoven.

Splice To cut and join together two pieces of film.

Sprocket The holes that run down the edges of film.

Tripod A three-legged stand to hold a camera steady.

Text Any medium offered to an audience. It can be a play, a film, an advertisement, a book, a radio programme, etc.

Uher Ultra high efficiency recorder. A reel-to-reel tape recorder offering precise editing with exceptional clarity.

Resources

The following addresses may be able to supply you with information, teaching packs, films for hire etc; there are also some suggestions for school visits.

BBC School Television, Villiers House, Ealing Broadway, London W5 2PA, tel. 01 743 8000 (some books and information available).
British Film Institute, Educational Department, 21 Stephens Street, London W1P 1PL tel. 01 255 1444 (Produces various teaching packs).
CFL Vision, PO Box 35, Wetherby, West Yorkshire, LS23 7EX (Hires and sells films, videos and tape-slide presentations).
Edinburgh Film Workshop Trust, 29 Albany Street, Edinburgh, EH1 3QN tel. 031 557 5242 (Video entitled *Nothing's Impossible*, which deals with the making of animated films, including projects with young people and people with special needs).
The English Centre, Ebury Teachers' Centre, Sutherland Street, London SW1 tel. 01 821 8011. (*Front Page News*, a pack giving detailed instructions for work on newspapers; also a booklet, *Making a Newspaper*).
Film Bank, Grayton House, 498-504 Fulham Road, London SW6 5NH tel. 01 386 9909 (Hires out feature films of all descriptions, including educational films).
ICI Schools Liaison Department, PO Box 6, Bessemer Road, Welwyn Garden City, Herts AL7 1HD tel. 0707 323400 (Resource calalogue available).
Media Education Centre, South Hill Park, Bracknell, Berks RG12 1BR tel. 0344 427272 (Several useful resources, including the magazine *Media Education*, an information pack on the film industry, and a video, *Teaching Media Matters*).
Media Education Centre, 5 Llandaff Road, Canton, Cardiff CF1 9NF tel. 0222 396 288 (S4C Media Pack, in Welsh and English, from Hughes Publishing (S4C) – ideas and techniques for media work).
Media Education Services, Quevain, Mold Road, Ewloe Green, Clwyd CH5 3AU tel. 0352 2121 (*Remix* – a primary media education resource pack by Linda McIver and Sue Williams).
Museum of the Moving Image (MOMI), Education Department, South Bank Centre, London SE1 8XT tel. 01 928 3535 (School visits and other resources).
National Musuem of Photography Film and Television, Princes View, Bradford, W.Yorks BD7 0TR tel. 0274 725 347 (School visits and other resources).
Sheffield Media Unit, Central Library, Surrey Street, Sheffield S1 1XZ tel. 0742 734746 (*The Television Programme*, by Stamp and Stone – a comprehensive guide to video work).
Slide Centre, Ilton, Ilminster, Somerset TA19 9HS tel. 04605 7151 (Sells slides and film strips).

Other Scholastic books

Teacher Handbooks
The *Teacher Handbooks* give an overview of the latest research in primary education, and show how it can be put into practice in the classroom. Covering all the core areas of the curriculum, the *Teacher Handbooks* are indispensable to the new teacher as a source of information and useful to the experienced teacher as a quick reference guide.

Management Books
The *Management Books* are designed to help teachers to organise their time, classroom and teaching more efficiently. The books deal with topical issues, such as *Parents and Schools* and organising and planning *Project Teaching*, and are written by authors with lots of practical advice and experiences to share.

Let's Investigate
Let's Investigate is an exciting range of photocopiable activity books giving open-ended investigative tasks. Designed to cover the six to twelve-year-old age range, these books are ideal for small group or individual work. Each book presents progressively more difficult concepts and many of the activities can be adapted for use throughout the primary school. Detailed teacher's notes outlining the objectives of each photocopiable sheet and suggesting follow-up activities have been included.

Acknowledgements

The author and publishers extend their thanks to the various schools and teachers who helped develop the activities in this book. Thanks are also due to the BFI working party.

Front and back cover artwork was supplied by Steve Hughes (Bradford Film Workshop) and children from Park Street Primary School, Cambridge; Quadring Cowley Primary School, Near Spalding, Lincolnshire; Rushton County Primary School, Kettering, Northamptonshire; Paston Ridings Infants School, Peterborough, Cambridgeshire; Wilmcote C of E Junior School, Near Stratford, Warwickshire.